COOKING WITH

BEER

AND

BOURBON

COOKING WITH
BEER
AND
BOURBON

HUNTER REED

120 Recipes with a KICK

© 2023 by Fox Chapel Publishing Company, Inc., 903 Square Street, Mount Joy, PA 17552.

Recipe selection, design, and book design © Fox Chapel Publishing. Recipes and photographs © G&R Publishing DBA CQ Products, unless otherwise noted.

The following images are credited to Shutterstock.com and their respective creators: page 9: L.O.N. Dslr Camera; page 10: Lapina Maria; page 11 and back cover, left: DenisProduction.com; page 12: Vladimir Gappov; pages 13, 23, 45, 51, 67, and 85: Africa Studio; beer glass icons throughout: Glitter_Klo; bourbon icons throughout: Ilya Bolotov; page 16: Eygeny Karandaev; page 19, right: Ellyy; page 19, left: Pogorelova Olga; page 20: JCDphoto; page 21 icons: A_KUDR, Antonov Maxim, Gabi Wolf, Gurza, Net Vector; page 22: Anne Richard; page 46: marcin jucha; page 59, bottom: MATTHEW J. WILLIAMS; page 61: Elena Veselova; page 86, top: K2 PhotoStudio; page 86, bottom: Brent Hofacker; page 98: aodaodaodaod; page 101, bottom: Igor Sh; page 102: Wirestock Creators.

ISBN 978-1-4971-0389-4

Library of Congress Control Number: 2023905492

To learn more about the other great books from Fox Chapel Publishing, or to find a retailer near you, call toll-free 800-457-9112 or visit us at *www.FoxChapelPublishing.com*.

We are always looking for talented authors. To submit an idea, please send a brief inquiry to acquisitions@foxchapelpublishing.com.

Printed in China
First printing

TABLE OF CONTENTS

48

58

66

74

INTRODUCTION

Beer and bourbon are delicious to drink, but also delicious when used in cooking.

Alcohol has been used in kitchens all throughout history. From wine and rum to vodka and liqueur, using alcohol in your recipes enhances the flavor profile of almost any dish you create. In this book, I'll be focusing on two that have the most warm, rich flavor profiles to work with: beer and bourbon.

Yes, beer and bourbon are delicious to drink by themselves, but did you know that it's actually very easy to add them to your everyday meals? In fact, cooking with beer and bourbon is widely known as a great way to add layers of seasoning, texture, and some of the most delicious aromas you could imagine. Use these liquids to create marinades, act as tenderizers, and insert buoyancy to your baked goods. You can also use beer instead of water, oil, and butter in most recipes.

And if you or one of your guests are alcoholic free, vegan, or gluten free, there are even tips and products that allow you to sip and cook without regret. There are plenty of breweries producing nonalcoholic, vegan, and gluten-free options, so no one has to go without a brew-infused bite. But more about that on page 21.

In this book, you will encounter the science, techniques, and recipes you need to cook with bourbon and beer like a pro. In the recipe section, search for the alcohol you want by color—I organized the mouth-watering appetizers, meals, and more by lightest to darkest alcohol type. And remember, you can substitute your favorite beer or bourbon in any of the recipes. I'll suggest to you what I think is best, but you might think up an amazing flavor combination that works just as well. Go for it!

The trick to cooking with alcohol is that it takes time to incorporate the deep, rich flavors into the dish you're preparing. So, make sure that you give yourself enough time to allow the beer or bourbon to reduce properly. It will be worth it when you smell the heavenly scents wafting through your house and see the smiles on your dinner guests' faces around the table. So, grab your favorite brew, make sure to read the safety precautions, and let's get cooking.

SAFETY

Alcohol is highly flammable, so keep that in mind when you use it in your cooking. Although it is safe to cook with, there are a few tips you need to keep in mind when dealing with alcohol and heat. It's always better to be prepared in the kitchen.

1. Avoid open flames. Don't pour alcohol into a pan that is over an open flame, like on a stove top. Instead, take the pan off the flame completely before pouring the liquid.

2. Use low heat. When cooking with alcohol, the liquid will evaporate, but don't turn up the heat to make it cook faster. This could result in unnecessary dangers to you and others. Set your heat setting to low and take your time.

3. Be careful. It's better to be safe than sorry when dealing with alcohol and flame. Don't leave your stove or pans unattended while you cook, and always make sure to have a fire extinguisher handy.

4. If your alcohol does catch fire, extinguish it safely. Don't use water. Instead, cover the pan with a lid, a damp dishcloth, or pour baking soda on top. Or, of course, using a fire extinguisher will do the trick.

Adding alcohol to a dish on the stove could be dangerous, so make sure you take the proper safety precautions.

COOKING WITH BEER AND BOURBON

Beer and bourbon are handy tools to creating the perfect sauce or reduction for your meal; by adding some liquid into the pan that was used to prepare meat, you can combine all the deliciousness together to make the perfect sauce. You can also use alcohol to enhance the texture of your baked goods. Who wouldn't want the fluffiest, tastiest, sweetest treats?

Whether cooking with beer, bourbon, or any other alcohol, one of the most important things to remember is to use the drink that has the best flavor to you. After reducing, simmering, marinating, and basting, the only thing remaining will be smells and tastes of the alcohol you choose—so don't cook with something you don't enjoy drinking! These tips will help you sort out all your options.

Adding beer to meat creates a rich, flavorful reduction or marinade.

COOKING WITH BEER

Beer is surprisingly helpful in the kitchen. Use it to marinate your meat, or add flavor and extra liquid to your favorite chili. Darker beers will have more flavor and punch than lighter beers, so it really depends on what you're in the mood for.

As you are surely aware, there are a wide variety of beers to choose from, whether in drinking or cooking. This book will cover the most common beer flavors and colors, but please note that there are more to discover, experiment with, and enjoy. I will suggest the best brew for each recipe, but feel free to pick whatever beer you'd like. In general, though, beer falls under two main categories: lager and ale. Let's take a closer look at the beer you'll be cooking with in this book. And remember, there are no rules—pick your favorite from each category. I'm not picky.

The carbonation in beer helps to create a light dough with delicious flavor.

Beer flavors and colors range from light to dark, with specific glasses for each type of brew. All are delicious, though!

Lager

Lager is made with bottom-fermenting yeast at cool temperatures, which gives it its crisp, light, and dry taste. Lagers also have a lower alcohol content, and not too many hops (an ingredient that contributes to the bitterness and stability of the beer).

American Pale Lager
This is the most popular style of beer in America (and the world). It is very low in malt flavor and has a crisp, dry, and light body. It is also highly carbonated.
Color: Pale
Alcohol Content: Between 3 and 5 percent
Glass: Pilsner
Examples: Budweiser, Heineken, Buckler (nonalcoholic), Bard's Lager (gluten free)

Pilsner
Pilsner is one of the world's most common beer styles. It is a pale lager and has a strong, hopped flavor with some spice.
Color: Ranges from pale straw to pale gold
Alcohol Content: Between 4 and 5.5 percent
Glass: Pilsner
Examples: Pilsner Urquell, AL's Classic Pilsner (nonalcoholic), New Grist (gluten free)

Light Lager
This beer has less calories because it contains less hops and barley. It does not have a malty aroma, and has instead a light, flowery scent. It is light-bodied and crisp.
Color: Pale straw
Alcohol Content: 2.5 to 3.5 percent
Glass: Mug
Examples: Bud Light, Coors Light, Miller Lite, Athletic Lite (nonalcoholic), American Light (gluten free)

Ale
Ale is made with top-fermenting yeast at warm temperatures. It tastes fruitier and sweeter, and has a fuller body. Ale tends to look darker and cloudier than lager and is well hopped.

Wheat Ale

Wheat ale, or German hefeweizen, are primarily brewed with wheat, rather than malted barley. This beer will have a citrusy taste and a cloudy look. There are several types to choose from, so pick your favorite!
Color: Can range from pale straw to light amber
Alcohol Content: Anywhere between 3.5 and 7 percent
Glass: Shaker pint or weizen
Examples: Samuel Adams Summer Ale, Blue Moon Belgian White, Weihenstephaner (nonalcoholic)

Pale Ale
This type of beer is brewed using mostly pale malts to give it a nice balance between the hop and malt flavors. Pale ales have a floral, fruity taste with clean, uncomplicated flavors.
Color: Pale gold
Alcohol Content: Anywhere between 4 and 7 percent
Glass: Shaker pint or tulip
Examples: Sierra Nevada Pale Ale, Partake (nonalcoholic), Omission Pale Ale (gluten free)

IPA
Also known as India Pale Ale, this beer is known for its bitterness, since it is brewed with a wide variety of hops. It has a floral, piney, citrusy hop aroma and flavor, and a bitterness to match.

Color: Ranges from pale gold to medium amber
Alcohol Content: Anywhere between 5.5 and 7.5 percent
Glass: Shaker pint or tulip
Examples: Founders Brewing Company, Juicy IPA by Two Roads Brewing (nonalcoholic), Buck Wild Hazy IPA (gluten free)

Amber Ale

Amber ale is brewed with malts to produce an amber color. It is quite balanced, with a variety of different flavors. Caramels and citrus flavors are common.

Color: Can vary between pale amber to deep red; any ales between pale ales and brown ales would fall here

Alcohol Content: Between 4 and 7 percent

Glass: Shaker pint

Examples: Great Lakes Brewing Company, O'Doul's Amber (nonalcoholic), Green's Discovery Amber Ale (gluten free)

Brown Ale

Any ale that is considered too dark to be amber ale and too light to be black ale fall here. (There are no recipes here that specifically call for a black ale, but you can try it out in dishes that require a malty, chocolatey taste.) Because of its wide range of strength, flavor, and hoppiness, it is very food friendly and can be paired with a wide variety of cuisines. Some brown ales can even have a stout-like chocolate and coffee flavor.

Color: Either light, dark, or medium brown, with possible reddish undertones

Alcohol Content: Between 4 and 8 percent

Glass: Nonic pint or shaker pint

Examples: Brooklyn Brown Ale, Imperial Nut Brown Ale, Sam's Brown Ale (nonalcoholic)

Porter

Porter is a dark beer, commonly flavored with coffee and chocolate to accentuate the roasted malt.

Color: Ranges from dark brown to black

Alcohol Content: Between 5 and 7.5 percent

Glass: Nonic pint or shaker pint

Examples: Alaskan Brewing Company, Surreal Nonalcoholic 17 Mile Porter (nonalcoholic), Burning Brothers Black Pepper Porter (gluten free)

Stout

Stout is a rich, dark brew that you can think of as porters with the dial turned up to nine or ten. It has a deep, roasted, strong taste with heavy chocolate and coffee notes.

Color: Ranges from deep brown to pitch black

Alcohol Content: Between 4 and 8 percent

Glass: Shaker pint or tulip

Examples: Guiness Extra Stout, Samuel Smith Oatmeal Stout, Grüvi Stout (nonalcoholic), Ghostfish Watchstander Stout (gluten free)

COOKING WITH BOURBON

In this book, I don't distinguish between the different types of bourbon like I do for beer. However, there are three main types of bourbon that you should consider when choosing your ingredients: traditional, mostly rye, and wheated.

Bourbon needs to be aged for at least two years to refine the rich, smoky flavors.

Traditional Bourbon

Traditional bourbon has equal portions barley and rye. It has a spiciness, but is also sweet with notes of caramel, oak, and vanilla.
Color: Rich amber
Alcohol Content: Between 40 and 50 percent
Glass: Glencairn
Examples: Wild Turkey, Evan Williams, Kentucky 74 (nonalcoholic)

Mostly Rye Bourbon

Mostly rye bourbon has double the rye and less corn and barley than traditional bourbon. Because of this, it is more spicy and less sweet, with notes of pepper.
Color: Rich amber
Alcohol Content: Between 40 and 50 percent
Glass: Glencairn

Examples: Redemption High Rye Bourbon, Jim Beam Signature Craft High Rye, Old Grand-Dad Bonded Bourbon

Wheated Bourbon

Wheated bourbon has almost the exact same recipe as traditional bourbon, but the rye is replaced with wheat. This produces a sweeter, smoother, and sugary bourbon.
Color: Rich amber
Alcohol Content: Between 40 and 50 percent
Glass: Glencairn
Examples: Maker's Mark, Larceny Small Batch, W.L. Weller Special Reserve

Once you've decided on your go-to brew, it's important to consider some additional aspects of cooking with bourbon before you start including it in our recipes.

1. Bourbon comes from barrels. Bourbon can't be aged in just any old barrel. The distilled clear liquor ("white dog") must go into a brand-new oak barrel—never a used one—that's been charred inside. Then it soaks for at least two years to pick up just the right natural caramel color and smoky flavor. If a batch of bourbon comes from one barrel—and only one—before being filtered, mixed with water, and bottled, it's a "single-barrel bourbon." Its flavor is unique to that barrel (and it's probably pricey). But big distillers mix many different barrels of bourbon together to get the consistent flavor they want. This means your favorite brand will taste the same every time you buy it.

What happens to the old bourbon barrels? They're reused to age other whiskeys and some dark beers. Barrel-aged beers pick up a natural flavor from those barrels that can't quite be copied by tossing toasted oak chips into steel barrels. But beer ages to perfection much faster than bourbon.

2. All bourbon is whiskey, but not all whiskey is bourbon. Official bourbon is only made in the USA and has at least 51% corn along with water, other grains, and yeast. Whiskeys like Scotch, Irish, and Tennessee can be distilled elsewhere, have added flavorings and colorings, and be aged or filtered differently.

3. Bourbon packs a punch. While beer can add different flavors to your dish like light citrus, dryness, or even bitterness, bourbon is most well-known for significantly adding intense smokiness, vanilla, and toasty nuttiness to your food. Just like with beer, though, only use bourbon that you would drink and enjoy.

If you don't like drinking it, you won't like eating it.

4. Use it in meats and marinades. No need to bring out the meat tenderizer; bourbon breaks down the enzymes in meat effortlessly, which not only softens the meat but also contributes to delicious marinades. Make sure to let it simmer, cooking off the alcohol and injecting the flavor as much as possible.

5. Find the balance. Since bourbon has such a strong flavor profile, be sure to not use too much or too little. You don't want to overpower the other flavors in the dish, but you also want to be able to taste it. Feel free to experiment until you find the perfect balance of bourbon tastiness.

Bourbon has an unmistakable flavor that elevates your cooking like no other ingredient.

THE SCIENCE OF COOKING WITH ALCOHOL

You may be wondering how including beer and bourbon in a dish could result in food that won't make you drunk. It all comes down to the science. Looking at the alcohol content in the beer and bourbon that is used in this book, you can see that beer has a low alcohol content to begin with. Once the alcohol cooks and simmers (the longer the better), the remaining alcohol content is minuscule. Bourbon starts out at a much higher alcohol content, so it must be cooked for longer. Just because it evaporates doesn't mean it's all gone! Take your time and let the alcohol simmer, reduce, and do its thing. In the meantime, let's take a closer look at some of the science of cooking with beer and bourbon.

Bourbon has carbonation, which contributes to the scientific benefits of cooking with alcohol.

Tip: Make guests aware of the alcoholic ingredients used in each dish. Although the remaining alcohol is minuscule, there are some people who may wish to avoid alcohol all together.

ALCOHOL RETENTION IN COOKING

When you pour your beer or bourbon into your hot pan (safely), you will immediately see some steam. The higher the temperature of the pan, the more steam you will see. But don't assume that means that the alcohol has burned off. Alcohol has a lower boiling point than water—173°F,

Alcohol has a lower boiling point than water, so when using beer to marinate meat, for example, burn at a lower temperature for a longer period of time to allow the alcohol to cook off and the flavors to remain behind

rather than 212°F—so when it starts to boil, the alcohol will begin to evaporate. However, it takes time and gradual heat to reduce that alcohol so that all it leaves behind is delicious tastes and smells. Cooking alcohol for a longer period of time in the oven or slow cooker will contribute to less alcohol retention in your final dish. And remember, our bodies naturally metabolize alcohol, so what little is leftover will not affect us other than making our mouths water.

This chart from the USDA shows what percentage of alcohol is retained after cooking it. You can then deduce that if you only reduce the alcohol by a small amount, there will be a higher amount of alcohol content leftover. So, it's probably a good idea to cook that alcohol for a long time. And anyway, it's always best to reduce the alcohol taste and make way for the wonderful flavor profiles of the drink that you lovingly paired with the dish.

Beer and bourbon are key ingredients in many well-loved dishes. And the best part is sipping while you cook.

CHEMICAL BREAKDOWNS AND BONDS

Since beer is saturated with CO_2, it easily breaks down fat much better than water does, which creates a lovely role in brining and marinating food. Alcohol in general does a great job at penetrating fatty meats, bringing along its own flavors that water just doesn't have.

Adding alcohol to your baking helps it chemically as well. Putting beer into batter helps it to expand quickly, thanks to the CO_2 inside beer, and since it does not need to cook as long as milk or water, the batter dries and crisps faster than normal. That's why beer-battered foods have such a delicious crunch while the inside meat or filling remains tender.

PERCENTAGE OF ALCOHOL REMAINING	
Stirred into hot liquid	85%
Flamed	75%
No heat, stored overnight	70%
Not stirred, but baked 25 minutes	45%
Stirred/Baked/ Simmered for 15 minutes	40%
Stirred/Baked/ Simmered for 30 minutes	35%
Stirred/Baked/ Simmered for 1 hour	25%
Stirred/Baked/ Simmered for 1.5 hours	20%
Stirred/Baked/ Simmered for 2 hours	10%
Stirred/Baked/ Simmered for 2.5 hours	5%

BEER AND BOURBON PAIRINGS

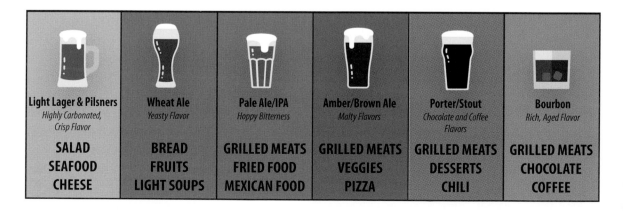

A dark porter or stout goes decadently with a rich, chocolate dessert.

Just like when you're thinking about what flavors should go together on your plate, pairing your beer and bourbon with the correct food is important. Whether you are picking the perfect brew to go alongside your meal or deciding which to include inside your recipe, use these tips to guide you to the perfect pair.

A general rule of thumb when it comes to flavor pairing is the lighter the dish, the lighter the alcohol. So, while this chart suggests the best pairings, you may want to switch things up if your recipe is calling for a darker, smoother flavor than it usually falls under. For example, fish is a light meat, usually paired best with pale lager or pilsner. However, if you are preparing fish and chips, which require a darker alcohol, you might want to pair it with a brown or amber ale. So, it really is about experimentation. Food is fun, isn't it?

It's also important to remember that since bourbon has such rich, deep flavors, the best contrast is citrusy, acidic foods. Sometimes the best pairing is something that balances out the flavor instead of matching it exactly. Another example is in dressings or sauces—if the recipe calls for bourbon, be prepared to combat that intense flavor with something acidic.

Light Lager & Pilsners *Highly Carbonated, Crisp Flavor*	Wheat Ale *Yeasty Flavor*	Pale Ale/IPA *Hoppy Bitterness*	Amber/Brown Ale *Malty Flavors*	Porter/Stout *Chocolate and Coffee Flavors*	Bourbon *Rich, Aged Flavor*
SALAD SEAFOOD CHEESE	BREAD FRUITS LIGHT SOUPS	GRILLED MEATS FRIED FOOD MEXICAN FOOD	GRILLED MEATS VEGGIES PIZZA	GRILLED MEATS DESSERTS CHILI	GRILLED MEATS CHOCOLATE COFFEE

NONALCOHOLIC, GLUTEN-FREE, AND VEGAN OPTIONS

You might be wondering: What about nonalcoholic, vegan, and gluten-free beer and bourbon options? Not to fear. The market is full of substitutions and products made specifically for you. And if you're not sure about buying a new product, there are

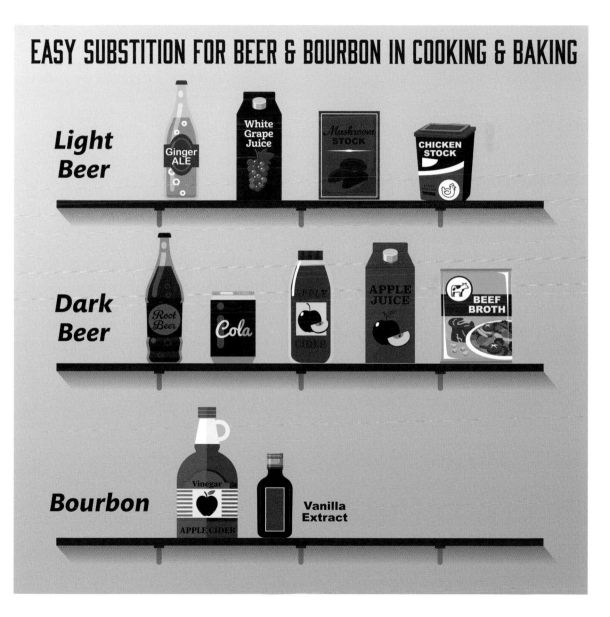

EASY SUBSTITION FOR BEER & BOURBON IN COOKING & BAKING

Light Beer

Ginger ALE · White Grape Juice · Mushroom STOCK · CHICKEN STOCK

Dark Beer

Root Beer · Cola · APPLE CIDER · APPLE JUICE · BEEF BROTH

Bourbon

APPLE CIDER Vinegar · Vanilla Extract

easy substitutions that might even be in your pantry. For light beer, try white grape juice, and for dark beer, give beef broth a try to mimic the flavor. When it comes to what the beer and bourbon chemically do to the ingredients while cooking, using a soda substitute (like ginger ale, cola, or root beer) will help break down meat and add carbonation to bread.

NONALCOHOLIC BEERS AND BOURBONS

Substitute any type of beer or bourbon for a nonalcoholic alternative and the recipe will stay delicious. However, if you are picking a nonalcoholic beer that has a bitter flavor, that bitterness will likely be accentuated in your dish because of how the nonalcoholic beer is made. Ginger ale, root beer, or beef broth can also be a great substitution. Or, if you want to substitute bourbon, vanilla extract and apple cider vinegar can mimic the taste.

Tip: Even if a beer is gluten free, double-check the recipe you're preparing to make certain you substitute flour or other gluten-containing ingredients for your gluten-free guests. Examples:
- Glutenberg Craft Brewery Blanche
- Angry Orchard Hard Cider
- White wine
- Chicken broth

GLUTEN-FREE BEERS AND BOURBONS

Just like with nonalcoholic beers and bourbons, there are plenty of gluten-free brands to choose from. Gluten is found in barley and wheat, which are two of the main ingredients of beer. So, when looking for gluten-free beer that is originally made with mostly wheat or barley, keep in mind that you might have a hard time finding a variety of options. Some ciders are also available gluten free, but just make sure to double-check the ingredients. Bourbon, on the other hand, is considered gluten-free because of its distillation process. If you're looking to substitute beer for something else, using soda or apple or white grape juice will give you the flavors and carbonation without the risk of contamination.

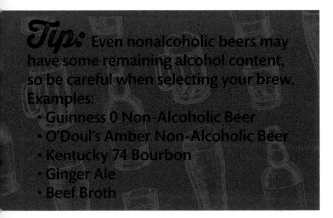

Tip: Even nonalcoholic beers may have some remaining alcohol content, so be careful when selecting your brew. Examples:
- Guinness 0 Non-Alcoholic Beer
- O'Doul's Amber Non-Alcoholic Beer
- Kentucky 74 Bourbon
- Ginger Ale
- Beef Broth

Glutenberg Craft Brewery is a popular gluten-free beer that you can pick up easily at the store.

VEGAN BEERS AND BOURBONS

The good news is that beer and distilled alcohol like bourbon have all-vegan ingredients. However, the bad news is that some breweries add finings that are not vegan to their beer, so be careful when selecting your brew. And similar to nonalcoholic and gluten-free beers, there are other ingredients you can substitute that are vegan, such as apple juice, mushroom stock, and white wine.

Many types of beer are naturally vegan, but double-check the ingredients to be sure there is no cross-contamination.

Tip: Just like with the gluten-free beers, make sure you double-check the recipe to make any necessary substitutions for your vegan guests. Vegans avoid meat, dairy, eggs, and honey, so be careful to adjust recipes to include them if they are coming for dinner or the big game.

Examples:
- Heineken
- Yuengling
- Mushroom Stock
- White Wine

APPETIZERS

Starting with American pale lager and working your way down to a dark porter, these appetizer recipes will cover everyone's palate at your party while also giving them a taste of what's to come. Read on to find delicious recipes for beer-infused party meatballs, fried pickles, and more.

**MAKES
32**

BEER BATTER FRIED MOZZARELLA STICKS

Ingredients

- **Oil for frying**
- **1 envelope onion soup mix**
- **1 cup all-purpose flour**
- **1 teaspoon baking powder**
- **2 eggs**
- **½ cup American pale lager**
- **1 tablespoon mustard**
- **16 mozzarella cheese sticks, unwrapped and cut in half**

1. In deep fat fryer, heat oil until the deep-fry thermometer reaches 375°.

2. Meanwhile, in a large bowl, beat onion soup mix, flour, baking powder, eggs, American pale lager, and mustard until smooth and well blended. Let batter stand 10 minutes.

3. Dip cheese in batter, and then carefully drop into hot oil. Fry, turning once, until golden brown; drain on paper towels. Serve warm with marinara sauce for dipping.

American Pale Lager

**MAKES
20**

BATTERED BUFFALO SHROOMS

Ingredients

- **1 pound white button mushrooms**
- **Canola oil**
- **2 cups all-purpose flour**
- **¾ cup milk**
- **1 egg**
- **½ teaspoon salt**
- **1 (12 ounce) bottle plus 2 tablespoons American pale lager, divided**
- **½ cup butter**
- **½ cup buffalo sauce**
- **1 teaspoon brown sugar**

1. Rinse and pat mushrooms dry. Line a rimmed baking sheet with foil and set a cooling rack over it. Heat 2 inches of canola oil to 350° in a heavy saucepan.

2. In a large bowl, mix flour, milk, egg, salt, and 1 bottle of American pale lager until smooth.

3. Dip the mushrooms into the batter and carefully set them into the hot oil. Fry until brown on all sides and transfer to the cooling rack. Repeat with the remaining mushrooms.

4. For the dipping sauce, melt butter in a small saucepan over medium heat. Stir in buffalo sauce, 2 tablespoons of American pale lager, and brown sugar. Simmer 1 to 2 minutes.

American Pale Lager

MOSCOW SHANDY

Ingredients

- **6 ounces American pale lager**
- **4 ounces ginger beer**
- **1 ounce vodka**
- **Juice of ½ lime**
- **¼ teaspoon freshly grated ginger**

SERVES 1

Perfect Pairing

Try these cocktails crafted with complementary alcohol. It's a match made in heaven.

Combine liquid ingredients in a cocktail glass. Add ginger to the glass and stir to combine. Add ice to fill and garnish with a slice of lime. Delicious!

BEERY MARY

Ingredients

- **Coarse sea salt**
- **6 ounces tomato juice**
- **Juice of ¼ lime, plus 1 lime wedge**
- **1 dash hot sauce**
- **1 dash Worcestershire sauce**
- **½ teaspoon celery salt**
- **6 ounces pilsner**
- **Olives**

Rub the rim of a pint glass with a lime wedge; dip into coarse sea salt. In the glass, combine tomato juice, lime juice, hot sauce, Worcestershire sauce, celery salt, and pilsner. Stir and add ice to fill. Garnish with lime wedge and olives.

Pilsner

SERVES 1

BEER BRAT POTATO NACHOS

Ingredients

- 1 pound bratwurst
- 2 (12 ounce) cans American pale lager
- 1 cup cream cheese
- 2 cups shredded cheddar cheese
- ¼ teaspoon garlic salt
- ¼ teaspoon cayenne pepper
- 2 tablespoons Dijon mustard
- ½ tablespoon black pepper
- ¼ teaspoon salt
- 1 (8 ounce) bag kettle-cooked potato chips
- 1 cup sauerkraut, drained and squeezed
- ½ cup Flamin' Beer Jalapeños (recipe below)
- Chopped chives

1. In a large skillet, brown the bratwurst on both sides over medium-high heat.

2. Add both cans of American pale lager to the skillet; simmer over medium-low heat for 20 minutes. Remove the bratwurst from the skillet, slice, and set aside.

3. Continue to simmer the beer over medium-low; add the cream cheese and cheddar cheese to the skillet. Stir occasionally until mixture is smooth.

4. Add the garlic salt, cayenne pepper, mustard, black pepper, and salt; stir to incorporate.

5. Spread the chips on a serving platter and top with the beer cheese, bratwurst slices, sauerkraut, and Flamin' Beer Jalapeños; garnish with chives.

India Pale Ale

FLAMIN' BEER JALAPEÑOS

Ingredients

- 5 to 6 jalapeños, thinly sliced
- 2 cloves garlic
- 1 cup IPA
- 1 cup apple cider vinegar
- 3 tablespoons sugar
- 2 teaspoons salt
- 1 tablespoon black peppercorns

1. Add the jalapeños and garlic to a glass jar.

2. In a saucepan over medium heat, combine the rest of the ingredients; stir until the salt and sugar dissolve.

3. Remove from heat and pour the pickling liquid over the jalapeños.

4. Cover and refrigerate for 24 hours. The jalapeños will last for several weeks in the refrigerator.

American Pale Lager

SERVES
6

MAKES
30

TIPSY FRIED PICKLES

Ingredients

- **1 egg**
- **1 teaspoon baking soda**
- **1 teaspoon paprika**
- **1 ¼ cup flour, divided**

- **Salt and black pepper, to taste**
- **¼ cup plus 2 tablespoons pilsner**
- **30 dill pickle spears, drained and patted dry**
- **Ranch dressing, for dipping**

1. Line a pan with foil and set a cooking rack over it.

2. Beat the egg in a medium bowl until frothy. Stir in baking soda, paprika, 1 cup of flour, and salt and black pepper. Gradually add pilsner; whisk until the batter is smooth.

3. Put ¼ cup flour in a zippered plastic bag, add a few pickle spears, zip to close, and shake until coated; remove the pickles. Repeat until you've coated all 30 pickles.

4. Heat 2 inches of canola oil to 350° in a deep-fryer or heavy saucepan.

5. Coat a few pickles in batter and carefully set them in the hot oil. Fry until brown on all sides and transfer to the cooling rack. Repeat with the remaining pickles. Serve with ranch dressing for dipping.

BEER-BQ PARTY MEATBALLS

Ingredients

- 1 cup panko breadcrumbs
- 2 pounds lean ground beef
- 1 ½ teaspoons minced garlic
- 2 eggs, beaten
- 1 tablespoon Worcestershire sauce
- 1 teaspoon black pepper
- 2 ½ teaspoons salt, divided
- 1 cup Bourbon "Q" Sauce (recipe found on page 94)
- 1 cup light lager
- 1 teaspoon sriracha sauce

1. Preheat the oven to 375° and line a couple of rimmed baking sheets with foil; coat with cooking spray and set aside.

2. Put the panko breadcrumbs into a large bowl and add ground beef, garlic, eggs, Worcestershire sauce, black pepper, and 2 teaspoons salt. Mix with your hands.

3. Use a level measuring tablespoon to form the meatballs, roll them in your hands to round them out, and then arrange them in the prepped pans.

4. In a bowl, whisk together Bourbon "Q" Sauce, light lager, sriracha sauce, and ½ teaspoon salt. Pour this evenly over the meatballs and bake 40 to 45 minutes.

Light Lager

MAKES
ABOUT
58

SERVES A CROWD!

BEER & PRETZEL CHEESE BALL

Ingredients

- 2 (8 ounce) packages cream cheese, softened
- 2 cups finely shredded Mexican cheese blend
- 1 (1 ounce) package dry ranch dip mix
- ½ cup pretzel wheat ale
- 5 bacon strips, cooked and crumbled
- 1 (2 ounce) jar pimentos, drained
- 3 green onions, sliced
- ½ cup pretzels, crushed, plus pretzels for serving

1. Beat cream cheese in a mixing bowl on medium speed until light and fluffy. Beat in Mexican cheese blend and ranch dip mix. Slowly pour in beer and continue mixing until well blended. Stir in the bacon, pimentos, and green onions.

2. Line a small bowl with plastic wrap, letting the ends hang over the edges; pack in the cheese mixture so it takes the shape of the bowl, flattening the top. Wrap the ends of the plastic over the cheese and set in the fridge for several hours.

3. When it's chilled, remove the cheese from the bowl and take off the plastic. Press the crushed pretzels all over the sides of the cheese ball. Serve with pretzels for dipping.

CHEESY BEER PUFFS

Ingredients

- **1 ¼ cups shredded cheddar**
- **¼ cup cream cheese**
- **¼ cup amber ale**
- **1 teaspoon bourbon**
- **1 teaspoon paprika**

- **1 teaspoon garlic powder**
- **Salt and pepper, to taste**
- **1 (17 ounce) package puff pastry, thawed**
- **1 egg**
- **1 tablespoon water**

1. Preheat oven to 425°. Line a rimmed baking sheet with parchment paper.

2. In a food processor, pulse cheddar, cream cheese, amber ale, bourbon, paprika, and garlic powder, scraping the bowl occasionally. Season with salt and black pepper.

3. Unfold the sheets from the puff pastry. Cut each sheet into nine 3-inch squares. Spoon some cheese mixture onto half of each pastry square, leaving a ½-inch rim.

4. Beat the egg with water and brush a little on the rim of a pastry square. Fold the square in half to form a triangle; seal the edges with the tines of a fork. Repeat with the remaining pastry squares.

5. Transfer to the baking sheet and brush with the egg mixture. Bake for 20 minutes or until golden brown.

Amber Ale & Bourbon

MAKES
18

FLATBREAD APPETIZERS

Ingredients

- 2 tablespoons unsalted butter
- ¼ cup olive oil, divided
- 2 sweet white onions, sliced
- Salt, to taste
- Sugar
- 1 cup porter
- 2 (6.5 ounce) packages pizza crust mix

- ½ teaspoon garlic salt
- 1 cup brown ale
- 2 ¼ cups shredded smoked Gouda cheese
- 1 ½ cups grape or cherry tomatoes, sliced
- ½ teaspoon black pepper
- 2 tablespoons fresh parsley, chopped

1. Melt together the butter and 2 tablespoons oil in a big saucepan over medium-low heat. Add the onions and a pinch of both salt and sugar; cover and cook 10 to 15 minutes, until softened.

2. Stir in the porter and cook until nearly evaporated and the mixture becomes glaze-like, all the while sipping the leftover porter and stirring the onions.

3. Preheat the oven to 400° and cover two rimmed baking sheets with parchment paper.

4. In a big bowl, combine the crust mix and garlic salt. Microwave the brown ale on high for 20 seconds or until warmed to 110°; pour into the bowl, stirring until dough forms. Cover and let stand 5 minutes.

5. Divide the dough into six equal pieces; flour lightly and press each into a 6-inch circle on the prepped baking sheets. Prebake the crusts about 3 minutes. Top with the Gouda and caramelized onions.

6. In a bowl, mix the tomatoes with the remaining 2 tablespoons oil, black pepper, and a little salt; divide among the crusts. Brush exposed dough with any oil remaining in the bowl. Bake for 15 to 20 minutes, until the crusts have turned a light golden brown.

7. Sprinkle with parsley and cut into appetizer-size servings.

SERVES
8

SIDES & SNACKS

Whether you serve these recipes with a main dish or just have them around to snack on while you're cooking dinner or watching the game, these snacks and sides will make your mouth water. Feel free to pair them with other dishes in this book, too!

American Pale Lager

SERVES
4

CHEESY BEER MASHED POTATOES

Ingredients

- **4 medium Yukon gold potatoes**
- **¼ cup American pale lager**
- **½ teaspoon garlic salt**
- **2 tablespoons butter**
- **¼ cup sour cream**
- **½ cup shredded cheddar cheese**
- **2 tablespoons chives, chopped**
- **Salt and pepper, to taste**

Perfect Pairing
These potatoes are the perfect pair to the Porter Pot Roast on page 102.

1. Peel and cut the potatoes into quarters and place them in a large saucepan; add enough water to cover. Bring to a boil and reduce heat to medium-low; cover loosely and boil gently for 15 to 20 minutes or until the potatoes are tender.

2. Drain and mash potatoes until no lumps remain.

3. Add American pale lager in small amounts, beating after each addition. Add garlic salt, butter, sour cream, shredded cheddar cheese, and chives.

4. Mash until potatoes are light and fluffy. Season with salt and black pepper

BREWER'S BEANS

Ingredients

- ½ pound bacon, chopped
- 1 pound lean ground beef
- ½ cup white onion, chopped
- 1 (16 ounce) can black beans, drained and rinsed
- 1 (16 ounce) can kidney beans, drained and rinsed
- 1 (16 ounce) can baked beans
- ½ cup packed brown sugar
- 1 cup American pale lager
- ⅓ cup ketchup
- 2 teaspoons apple cider vinegar
- 1 teaspoon Dijon mustard
- 1 teaspoon chipotle powder
- ¼ teaspoon garlic powder
- ¼ teaspoon black pepper

Perfect Pairing

These served with the Bubblin' Beer Dogs on page 86 leads to some happy guests.

SERVES 8

1. In a large skillet, cook the bacon over medium heat until crisp. Transfer to paper towels to drain and cool; discard the drippings.

2. In the same skillet, cook the beef and onion over medium heat until the meat is no longer pink; drain the drippings.

3. In a large bowl, stir together the beef mixture, bacon, beans, brown sugar, American pale lager, ketchup, vinegar, mustard, chipotle powder, garlic powder, and black pepper.

4. Transfer to a 9″ x 13″ baking dish and bake, uncovered, at 325° for 45 to 60 minutes or until the beans are as soft as desired.

BACON-BEER GREEN BEANS

Perfect Pairing

This is the perfect side for the Irresistible Bourbon Salmon, found on page 83.

Pilsner

SERVES 4

Ingredients

- **6 bacon strips**
- **1 (16 ounce) package frozen cut green beans**
- **⅓ cup pilsner**
- **⅓ cup butter, cut into small pieces**
- **3 tablespoons brown sugar**
- **3 tablespoons distilled white vinegar**
- **4 teaspoons cornstarch**
- **2 teaspoons white onion, finely chopped**

1. Cook, drain, and crumble bacon; set aside.
2. In a saucepan, combine green beans, pilsner, and butter; bring to a boil over medium heat. Reduce the heat to low, cover, and simmer for 6 to 8 minutes or until crisp-tender. Remove the beans with a slotted spoon, keeping the liquid in the saucepan.
3. To the saucepan, add brown sugar, distilled white vinegar, cornstarch, and white onion; stir until well blended. Bring to a boil and cook for a minute or two, until thickened.
4. Stir in the beans and heat through. Sprinkle with set-aside bacon.

Light Lager

SERVES 6

BEER-SIMMERED CORN

Ingredients

- **4 (12 ounce) bottles light lager**
- **3 tablespoons butter**
- **½ teaspoon salt**
- **½ teaspoon seafood seasoning**
- **6 ears corn**

Perfect Pairing

These taste so good with the Beer-Doused Burgers on page 96.

1. Bring the light lager to boil in a large pot. Add butter, salt, and seafood seasoning. Add corn and reduce heat to low.
2. Cover and cook, turning occasionally, until corn is tender, about 15 minutes.
3. Serve with butter, salt, black pepper, and lime wedges for drizzling

SERVES 6

BEER-BRAISED BRUSSELS

Ingredients

- 2 pounds brussels sprouts
- 8 bacon strips, chopped
- 1 shallot, thinly sliced
- 1 (12 ounce) bottle amber ale
- ½ teaspoon salt
- ¼ teaspoon black pepper
- 1 tablespoon honey
- ¼ teaspoon crushed red pepper

1. Wash and trim the ends off the brussels sprouts; cut them in half and set aside.

2. Add the bacon to a large skillet over medium heat and sauté until crisp; drain the drippings and set the bacon aside to cool.

3. Add the shallot to the skillet and sauté for 2 to 3 minutes to soften, then add the brussels sprouts. Sauté for 4 to 5 minutes.

4. Pour the amber ale into the skillet. Add the salt, pepper, honey, and crushed red pepper. Bring to a simmer and lower the heat.

5. Stir and simmer until the beer has reduced to a glaze and the sprouts are cooked through, about 15 minutes.

6. Chop the bacon and stir into the mixture. Serve and enjoy!

ALE-GLAZED CARROTS & WALNUTS

Amber Ale

Ingredients

- **1 pound fresh carrots**
- **3 tablespoons butter**
- **1 cup amber ale**
- **1 tablespoon maple syrup**
- **½ cup walnut halves**

Perfect Pairing
This side pairs well with Chicken Beer-sala, found on page 100.

SERVES
4

1. Wash and peel carrots; cut into ½-inch slices.

2. Melt butter in a large saucepan over medium heat. Add the carrots and amber ale and bring to a boil. Reduce heat so the beer bubbles gently; add maple syrup.

3. Simmer for 15 minutes, stirring occasionally, until the carrots are almost cooked through.

4. Stir in walnuts and cook for 5 more minutes, or until the glaze is reduced to a couple of tablespoons.

Amber Ale

SWEET POTATO ALE FRIES

Ingredients

- **3 pounds sweet potatoes**
- **1 (12 ounce) can amber ale**
- **2 tablespoons olive oil**
- **1 teaspoon minced garlic**
- **1 teaspoon dried rosemary**
- **1 teaspoon salt**
- **½ teaspoon black pepper**

Perfect Pairing
Pair these with Rosemary Beer Chicken from page 97. The perfect meal.

SERVES
6

1. Preheat oven to 450°.

2. Scrub sweet potatoes and cut into ½-inch slices; cut the slices into french fry shapes.

3. In a large bowl, soak the cut fries in amber ale for 20 minutes, tossing 1 or 2 times. Drain the beer and toss the fries with olive oil, garlic, rosemary, salt, and pepper until well coated.

4. Spread a single layer of fries on a rimmed baking sheet. Bake for 45 minutes to 1 hour, depending on how crispy you like them, turning 2 or 3 times.

BREWPUB MAC

Ingredients

- 8 bacon strips, chopped
- 1 (16 ounce) box macaroni
- ¼ cup butter
- 1 teaspoon minced garlic
- ¼ cup all-purpose flour
- 1 teaspoon salt
- ½ teaspoon black pepper
- ½ teaspoon paprika
- 2½ cups milk
- 1 cup amber ale
- ¼ cup heavy cream
- 2 cups shredded Gouda cheese
- 2 cups shredded cheddar cheese
- Chives, for topping

1. Add bacon to a large skillet over medium heat; sauté until crisp and set aside to drain.

2. Cook macaroni according to package directions for al dente; drain and set aside.

3. In a large pot, melt butter over medium-high heat. Add garlic, flour, salt, black pepper, and paprika, stirring until smooth. Whisk in milk, amber ale, and heavy cream. Bring to a boil and stir until thickened.

4. Reduce heat. Add cheeses and stir until melted. Add the macaroni and half the crumbled bacon and stir to combine.

5. Top with the remaining bacon and chives.

Amber Ale

SERVES
4

Bourbon

MAKES
2½
CUPS

COCKTAIL-INSPIRED PECANS

Ingredients

- ¼ cup dried cherries
- ¼ cup bourbon
- 2 tablespoons brown sugar
- 1 teaspoon salt
- ¼ teaspoon black pepper
- ¼ teaspoon cayenne pepper
- 2 cups pecan halves
- 2 tablespoons unsalted butter
- 1 tablespoon orange zest

Perfect Pairing
Snack on these by themselves, or toss them on top of the Bacon & Ale Pecan Salad on page 74.

1. Soak the dried cherries in the bourbon for at least 1 hour.

2. In a small bowl, stir together the brown sugar, salt, black pepper, and cayenne. Line a rimmed baking sheet with parchment paper. Set aside.

3. To toast the pecans, put them in a single layer in a large nonstick skillet over medium heat for about 8 minutes or until they just start to look a little toasty, stirring often. Drop the butter into the hot skillet with the toasted pecans, letting it melt; stir to fully coat the pecans. Sprinkle the set-aside sugar mixture evenly over the pecans and stir again to coat. Take the skillet off the heat and stir in the cherries and the bourbon they were soaking in.

4. Return the pan to the heat for a few minutes, until the liquid is absorbed and the pecans are nicely glazed.

5. Spread evenly on the prepped baking sheet to let cool. Once cool to the touch, sprinkle pecans with the orange zest.

SERVES
6

BOURBON MAC & CHEESE

Perfect Pairing
Pair this with Bourbon Street
Chicken on page 105 for the
perfect comfort meal.

Ingredients

- ½ cup plus 1 tablespoon bourbon, divided
- ¾ cup brown sugar
- 1 teaspoon cayenne pepper
- 10 bacon strips
- 1 pound large elbow macaroni, uncooked
- 3 tablespoons unsalted butter
- ⅓ cup flour
- 2 cups milk
- 3 cups shredded sharp cheddar cheese
- 1 cup shredded provolone cheese
- ½ teaspoon paprika
- Salt and black pepper, to taste

1. Preheat the oven to 400° and line a rimmed baking sheet with foil; coat the foil with cooking spray and set aside.

2. Bring ½ cup bourbon to a boil in a small saucepan. Reduce the heat and simmer until reduced to just 2 or 3 tablespoons.

3. Mix the brown sugar and cayenne on a plate and dredge both sides of the bacon in it, pressing well to adhere; arrange on the prepped baking sheet and bake for 7 minutes; flip and bake 5 minutes more or until almost crisp. Transfer to a greased plate to cool, then chop and set aside.

4. Cook macaroni to al dente according to package directions; drain and set aside.

5. Melt the butter in a saucepan over medium-high heat; whisk in the flour until blended. Whisk in the reduced bourbon and the remaining 1 tablespoon bourbon until smooth.

6. Slowly whisk in the milk; cook until it thickens, stirring often. Whisk in the cheddar and provolone (a handful at a time), paprika, salt, and black pepper until cheese melts. Pour over macaroni and add the bacon.

SAUCES & DIPS

The recipes in this section incorporate delicious beer and bourbon into sauces, dressing, and dips that perfectly accompany a beer- or bourbon-infused entrée as well as a meal or snack made without alcohol. Pair these sauces and dips with crunchy crackers or chips and let the deliciousness begin.

BEER CHEESE PRETZEL & DIP

Ingredients

- 1 (16 ounce) package hot bread roll mix with yeast
- 1 cup shredded sharp cheddar cheese
- 1¼ cup pilsner, plus ½ cup, divided
- 1 egg, beaten

- 2 tablespoons kosher salt
- 1 (8 ounce) package cream cheese, diced and softened
- 1 (8 ounce) package processed cheese, cubed
- ¾ teaspoons garlic powder

1. Preheat oven to 350°. In a medium bowl, mix the hot bread roll mix with yeast and cheddar cheese.

2. In a microwave or small saucepan, heat 1¼ cups of pilsner to almost boiling.

3. Stir pilsner and egg into the flour mixture and knead for 5 minutes.

4. Allow the dough to rest for 5 minutes, then roll into desired pretzel shape. Sprinkle with kosher salt. Bake 25 minutes in the preheated oven or until golden brown.

5. **For the dip:** In food processor, blend the cream cheese, processed cheese, garlic powder, and remaining ½ cup room-temperature pilsner. Refrigerate until serving with pretzels.

Pilsner

SERVES
4

MAKES
3
CUPS

SPIKED SALSA

Ingredients

- **5 Roma tomatoes**
- **2 jalapeños**
- **1 garlic clove**
- **½ cup white onion, chopped**
- **½ cup light lager**
- **1 teaspoon salt**
- **¼ teaspoon black pepper**
- **Juice of 2 limes**
- **½ cup cilantro, chopped**
- **Tortilla chips, for dipping**

1. Preheat a skillet to medium-high; place tomatoes and jalapeños in the skillet and roast for 3 minutes.

2. Add garlic and white onion to the skillet; continue roasting the vegetables, turning occasionally, until they become slightly charred and soft. Let the vegetables cool slightly before removing the stems from the jalapeños; if you prefer a milder salsa, remove the seeds and membranes as well.

3. Transfer the charred vegetables to a food processor; add light lager, salt, black pepper, and lime juice. Pulse until the mixture is coarsely chopped.

4. Stir in cilantro and serve with tortilla chips.

HARVEST CHEESE DIP

Ingredients

- 3 tablespoons unsalted butter
- 3 tablespoons flour
- ¾ cup pumpkin ale
- ¾ cup apple juice
- ¾ cup pumpkin purée
- 2 tablespoons Dijon mustard
- ½ teaspoon pumpkin pie spice
- ½ teaspoon garlic powder
- ½ teaspoon cayenne pepper
- ½ teaspoon salt
- 6 ounces cream cheese, cubed
- 3 ½ cups shredded sharp cheddar cheese
- 4 bacon strips, cooked and crumbled
- 2 tablespoons chives, chopped
- Tortilla chips, for dipping

1. Melt butter in a saucepan over medium heat. Whisk in the flour and cook for 2 minutes. Add the pumpkin ale, apple juice, pumpkin purée, and mustard, whisking to blend. Bring to a simmer and heat for 5 minutes or until thickened.

2. Stir in the pie spice, garlic powder, cayenne, and salt. Add the cream cheese and stir until melted. Add the cheddar cheese (½ cup at a time), making sure each addition is completely melted before adding the next.

3. Carefully take a little taste and adjust the seasonings.

4. Transfer the dip to a serving bowl or small slow cooker set on low to keep warm; sprinkle with the bacon and chives. Serve immediately with tortilla chips.

SERVES A CROWD!

ORANGE-ALE VINAIGRETTE

Ingredients

- ¼ cup plus 2 tablespoons IPA
- 1 tablespoon shallot, finely chopped
- 1 teaspoon orange zest
- 1 tablespoon plus 1 teaspoon honey
- 1 teaspoon Dijon mustard
- ¼ cup olive oil
- Salt and pepper, to taste

In a blender, process IPA, shallot, orange zest, honey, and mustard until combined. With the motor running, gradually add olive oil in a thin stream until well mixed. Season with salt and pepper and serve over mixed greens.

India Pale Ale

MAKES
½
CUP

India Pale Ale

MAKES
2
CUPS

HOT & HOPPED HUMMUS

Ingredients

- 2 jalapeños, stemmed and seeded
- 3 tablespoons tahini paste
- 1 ½ cups canned garbanzo beans, drained and rinsed
- ⅓ cup cilantro, chopped
- 1 tablespoon olive oil
- Juice of 1 lime
- ½ teaspoon minced garlic
- ½ teaspoon onion powder
- ½ teaspoon salt
- ½ teaspoon cayenne pepper
- ⅓ cup IPA
- Tortilla or pita chips, for dipping

Add all ingredients to a food processor. Process until smooth and well mixed. Serve with pita or tortilla chips for dipping.

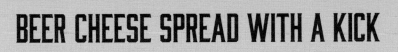

India Pale Ale

MAKES 2 CUPS

BEER CHEESE SPREAD WITH A KICK

Ingredients

- 1 (8 ounce) package shredded cheddar cheese
- 4 ounces cream cheese, softened
- ⅓ cup IPA
- 1 teaspoon Worcestershire sauce
- 1 teaspoon chili powder
- ½ teaspoon ground mustard
- ¼ teaspoon cayenne pepper
- 1 teaspoon dried parsley flakes
- Chips or bread, for dipping

1. In a blender or food processor, combine cheddar cheese, cream cheese, IPA, Worcestershire sauce, chili powder, ground mustard, and cayenne pepper. Process until well incorporated and smooth.

2. Add dried parsley flakes and mix just until blended. Remove from blender and place in a serving bowl.

3. Cover with plastic wrap and refrigerate or chill in cooler until ready to serve. Serve with chips or bread.

CHEESY BEER & SPINACH DIP

Ingredients

- ⅔ cup brown ale
- 3 cups shredded Monterey Jack cheese
- 2 tablespoons all-purpose flour
- ½ cup frozen chopped spinach, thawed and drained

- 1 tablespoon fresh cilantro, chopped
- Salt and pepper, to taste
- Tortilla chips, for dipping

1. In a medium saucepan over medium heat, bring brown ale to a boil. Lower heat.

2. Slowly stir in cheese and flour. Cook and stir until cheese is melted, but not bubbly.

3. Mix spinach, cilantro, salt, and pepper into the beer mixture. Serve warm with tortilla chips.

Brown Ale

MAKES
3
CUPS

SERVES A CROWD!

INE-BRIE-ATED ONION DIP

Ingredients

- 1 large Vidalia onion, thinly sliced
- 1 tablespoon unsalted butter
- 1 tablespoon olive oil
- ½ cup porter, divided
- 1 (8 ounce) package Brie cheese
- 1 teaspoon dried thyme

- 1 teaspoon fresh chives, chopped
- 1 tablespoon honey
- 1 (8 ounce) package cream cheese, softened
- 1 tablespoon cornstarch
- Baguette, sliced, for dipping

1. Put the onion into a pot over medium heat with the butter and olive oil. Cook until the onions start to soften, and then add ¼ cup porter.

2. Cook over medium heat, stirring occasionally, until the onions turn dark brown and the beer has evaporated. Add the additional beer and cook until the pot only has about 2 tablespoons of liquid left.

3. Trim the rind off the Brie and cut it into small cubes. Stir together the thyme, chives, honey, Brie, cream cheese, and cornstarch.

4. Bake at 375° for 15 minutes or until the cheese is bubbly; stir to combine. Serve warm with baguette slices.

SERVES A CROWD!

FIRECRACKER CHEESE SPREAD

Ingredients

- 8 ounces shredded smoked sharp cheddar cheese
- 8 ounces shredded apple-smoked white cheddar cheese
- 3 tablespoons bourbon
- ¼ cup pickled jalapeños
- 1 teaspoon salt
- ⅓ cup plus 2 teaspoons stout

In a food processor, combine all ingredients until everything is well blended and a spreading consistency. Transfer to a bowl. Serve with party rye bread, crackers (a roasted garlic flavor goes nicely), and veggies.

BREADS

These beer and bourbon bread recipes are light, fluffy, and have a delicious malty flavor. Even those who don't like the taste of beer or bourbon will enjoy these comforting, yeasty-flavored breads. Feel free to pair them with some of the soup and chili recipes starting on page 63 for extra levels of beer, bourbon, and bliss.

JALAPEÑO CHEDDAR BEER BREAD

Ingredients

- 3 cups all-purpose flour
- ¼ cup sugar
- ¼ teaspoon garlic salt
- 1 tablespoon baking powder
- 2 jalapeños
- 1 cup shredded cheddar cheese, divided
- 1 (12 ounce) bottle pilsner
- 8 tablespoons unsalted butter, melted
- ¼ cup Chipotle Beer Butter (see bleow)

1. Preheat oven to 350° and grease a 5″ x 9″ loaf pan.

2. Sift the flour into a large bowl; add the sugar, garlic salt, and baking powder and stir until combined.

3. Remove the seeds and membranes from the jalapeños, then add the peppers and ¾ cup cheddar cheese to the bowl. Pour the pilsner over the mixture and stir until well mixed.

4. Transfer the dough into the greased loaf pan and pour melted butter over the top. Bake for 30 minutes, then sprinkle with the remaining ¼ cup cheddar cheese and bake for 25 minutes more. Serve with Chipotle Beer Butter.

Pilsner

MAKES ¾ CUP

CHIPOTLE BEER BUTTER

Ingredients

- ½ cup butter, softened
- 2 chipotle peppers, minced
- 1 tablespoon adobo sauce
- 2 tablespoons pilsner
- Juice of 1 lime
- 1 tablespoon cilantro, chopped

With an electric mixer, whip butter until smooth and fluffy. Add chipotle peppers, adobo sauce, pilsner, lime juice, and cilantro to the mixture. Whip until incorporated. Serve with Jalapeño Cheddar Beer Bread.

Pilsner

SERVES
8

No Yeast Needed

The carbonation in the beer makes
the bread light and fluffy, which
means this is the easiest homemade
bread you'll ever make!

SERVES
4

LIQUID COURAGE CORNBREAD

Ingredients

- 1 cup all-purpose flour
- 1 cup cornmeal
- 4 teaspoons baking powder
- ½ teaspoon salt

- 1 egg
- ½ cup milk
- ½ cup light lager
- 2 tablespoons honey

1. Preheat the oven to 350°.

2. Combine flour, cornmeal, baking powder, and salt in a large bowl.

3. In a separate bowl, whisk together egg, milk, light lager, and honey; add to the cornmeal mixture and stir until just blended.

4. Pour into a greased 8″ x 8″ pan. Bake for 20 minutes or until the top is lightly browned and a toothpick inserted in the center comes out clean.

BEER-NANA BREAD

Bavarian-Style Wheat Ale

MAKES 1 LOAF

Ingredients

- 3 cups self-rising flour
- ¾ cup quick-cooking oats
- ½ cup brown sugar
- 1 ½ cups mashed ripe bananas
- ¼ cup pure maple syrup
- 1 (12 ounce) bottle Bavarian-style wheat ale
- 1 tablespoon sesame seeds
- ¼ teaspoon coarse salt

1. Preheat the oven to 375° and grease a 5″ x 9″ loaf pan.

2. In a bowl, mix flour, oats, and brown sugar.

3. In a separate bowl, stir together bananas, maple syrup, and Belgian-style wheat ale (you could also try a banana or banana bread beer).

4. Stir the flour mixture into the banana mixture until just moistened. Spread evenly into the prepped pan and sprinkle with sesame seeds and coarse salt.

5. Bake 55 to 60 minutes or until the bread tests done. Cool in pan 10 minutes before removing to a cooling rack.

BEER CHEESE BREAD WITH ONIONS

Wheat Ale

MAKES 1 LOAF

Ingredients

- 3 cups flour
- 1 tablespoon baking powder
- 1 ½ teaspoons salt
- 3 tablespoons sugar
- 1 cup cheddar cheese, grated
- 4 green onions, finely chopped
- 1 (12 ounce) can wheat ale

1. Combine flour, baking powder, salt, sugar, cheese, and onions.

2. Mix in wheat ale.

3. Pour in greased and floured loaf pan. Bake at 350° for 1½ hours.

Extra Pale Ale

MAKES
1
LOAF

GARLIC & HERB BEER BREAD

Ingredients

- **¼ cup butter, divided**
- **2 cups whole wheat flour**
- **1 cup all-purpose flour**
- **3 tablespoons sugar**
- **1 tablespoon baking powder**
- **1 teaspoon garlic powder**
- **1 teaspoon salt**
- **1 teaspoon dried rosemary**
- **1 teaspoon dried thyme**
- **1 teaspoon dried oregano**
- **1 (12 ounce) bottle extra pale ale**

1. Grease a 5″ x 9″ loaf pan with cooking spray and melt butter in the microwave; set both aside.

2. In a large bowl, mix the flours, sugar, baking powder, garlic powder, salt, rosemary, thyme, and oregano. Stir in the extra pale ale until just mixed.

3. Coat the bottom of the prepped pan with 2 tablespoons of the melted butter.

4. Spread the batter in the pan and brush the remaining 2 tablespoons butter over the top.

5. Bake for 50 minutes or until the bread tests done.

ITALIAN BEER BREAD

Ingredients

- 3 ½ cups bread flour, more if needed
- 2 teaspoons instant yeast
- 1 teaspoon fine sea salt
- 1 to 2 tablespoons minced Italian seasonings
- 1 ¼ cups diced cheese (Swiss, provolone, fontina, or cheddar)

- 3 tablespoons olive oil
- 2 tablespoons honey
- 12 ounces brown ale
- 1 egg white, beaten with 2 teaspoons water
- Fresh herbs, for topping

1. In a large bowl, thoroughly whisk together flour, yeast, and salt; if using herbs, whisk them in now. Add oil, honey, and brown ale. Stir with a spatula until well mixed.

2. If using a stand mixer, knead using the dough hook for 4 minutes on medium speed (or the manufacturer's recommended speed). If making by hand, turn the dough onto a lightly floured surface and knead for 8 to 10 minutes or until the dough becomes smooth and elastic. If the dough is too sticky to knead by hand, add up to ¼ cup more flour. Knead in other additions, such as cheese or bacon, at the end of the kneading.

3. Cover the dough with lightly greased plastic wrap or a damp towel and let rise until doubled—about 1 hour.

4. Gently flatten the dough and divide into thirds. Roll each piece under your hands into a 16-inch strand. Braid strands together on a parchment paper-lined or greased baking sheet, pinching ends together and tucking them under.

5. Cover and let rise about 30 minutes until nearly doubled. Preheat the oven to 375°F.

6. When the dough is ready, brush lightly with egg white. Bake for 25 to 30 minutes until golden-brown (if making rolls, reduce baking by 5 to 10 minutes). Sprinkle fresh herbs on top.

MAKES
1
LOAF

Brown Ale

SERVES
12

SKILLET BOURBON CORNBREAD

Ingredients

- 2 cups white flour
- 1 cup whole wheat flour
- 1 cup sugar
- 1 cup cornmeal
- 2 tablespoons baking powder
- 1 ½ teaspoons salt
- ½ cup bourbon
- 1 cup buttermilk
- 1 cup butter, melted and cooled
- 2 eggs, beaten
- Coarse ground black pepper

1. Preheat the oven to 350° and grease a 12-inch cast iron skillet.

2. In a medium bowl, stir together flours, sugar, cornmeal, baking powder, and salt.

3. In a separate bowl, whisk together bourbon, buttermilk, butter, and eggs; pour into the dry ingredients and stir until just combined.

4. Transfer to the skillet and sprinkle with pepper. Bake for 25 to 30 minutes or until it tests done.

Perfect Pairing

This tastes amazing when paired with Bourbon Chili on page 70.

CHILIS & SOUPS

You don't have to be a beer or bourbon lover to enjoy these rich, deep soups and chilis. Beer adds bold flavors and textures, and bourbon enhances the smoky flavors already found in the ingredients. Pair these soups with some delicious beer- and bourbon-enhanced bread (recipes starting on page 55), or even your favorite drink, and enjoy the warmth that comes with soon after.

Throwing A Fiesta?
Set out a variety of toppings and let guests top their own bowls.

SERVES
5

CERVEZA TORTILLA SOUP

Ingredients

- 1 (14.5 ounce) can fire-roasted diced tomatoes
- 1 (12 ounce) bottle American pale lager
- 4 cups chicken broth
- ½ teaspoon chipotle powder
- ½ teaspoon ground cumin
- ½ teaspoon onion powder
- 1 teaspoon chili powder
- 1 teaspoon garlic powder
- ½ teaspoon red pepper flakes
- ½ teaspoon salt
- 1 pound boneless, skinless chicken breasts
- Cilantro, avocado, cotija cheese, and tortilla chips, for topping

1. Put the tomatoes and American pale lager into a food processor and pulse until well combined.

2. Transfer the mixture to a large pot over medium-high heat along with the broth, chipotle powder, ground cumin, onion powder, chili powder, garlic powder, red pepper flakes, and salt. Bring to a simmer and add the chicken to the pot to cook.

3. Once the chicken is cooked through, about 20 minutes, shred the chicken and add it back to the soup.

4. Top each bowl of soup with cilantro, diced avocado, crumbled cotija cheese, and tortilla chips.

WHITE BEAN BEER CHILI

Ingredients

- **1 pound ground turkey**
- **1 white onion, chopped**
- **3 jalapeños, diced**
- **1 (12 ounce) bottle pilsner**
- **2 cups chicken broth**
- **4 (15 ounce) cans great northern beans, drained and rinsed**
- **¼ teaspoon garlic powder**
- **¼ teaspoon paprika**
- **½ teaspoon chipotle powder**
- **¼ teaspoon cumin**
- **¼ teaspoon chili powder**
- **¼ teaspoon oregano**
- **1 cup sour cream**
- **Salt and pepper, to taste**

1. Add the ground turkey to a large pot over medium heat; break into small pieces while cooking. Add onion and jalapeños; cook until softened.

2. Add pilsner and chicken broth, scraping to deglaze the pan. Add beans, garlic powder, paprika, chipotle powder, cumin, chili powder, and oregano. Simmer for 10 minutes.

3. Remove from heat, stir in sour cream, and season to taste with salt and black pepper. Ladle into bowls and top with shredded cheddar cheese and cilantro.

Pilsner

SERVES 8

SLOW & EASY STEAK & ALE SOUP

Ingredients

- 2 tablespoons olive oil, divided
- ¼ cup flour
- ½ teaspoon salt
- ½ teaspoon black pepper
- 1 pound chuck roast, trimmed and cut into bite-sized pieces
- 1 onion, sliced
- 1 to 2 cups mushrooms, sliced
- 1 celery rib, sliced
- 1 tablespoon minced garlic
- 2 large potatoes, cut into bite-sized pieces
- 1 (12 ounce) bottle extra pale ale, plus more for thinning
- 1 chicken bouillon cube
- ½ teaspoon dried thyme
- 1 (5 ounce) can evaporated milk
- 1 ½ cups shredded sharp cheddar cheese

1. Heat 1 tablespoon of the oil in a skillet over medium heat. Mix the flour, salt, and black pepper in a big, zippered plastic bag. Toss in the cubed meat and shake to coat.

2. Put the coated cubes in the hot oil and cook until browned on all sides, turning as needed. Transfer the browned meat to a 3-quart slow cooker.

3. Return the skillet to the heat and add the remaining 1 tablespoon oil. Add the onion, mushrooms, celery, and garlic and cook until the onions are crisp-tender; dump into the slow cooker along with the potatoes.

4. Add the beer, bouillon cube, and thyme. Cover and cook on high 3 ½ hours or until thickened and potatoes are tender.

5. Turn off the cooker and pour in the evaporated milk. Stir in the cheese, cover, and let set for 10 minutes or until the cheese is melted. Stir again before serving. For a thinner soup, stir in water or a little extra beer.

Extra Pale Ale

SERVES
4

India Pale Ale

SERVES
2

WISCONSIN CHEESE & BEER SOUP

Ingredients

- 2 tablespoons butter
- 2 tablespoons all-purpose flour
- 1 envelope onion soup mix
- 3 cups milk
- 1 teaspoon Worcestershire sauce

- 1 cup shredded cheddar cheese
- ½ cup IPA
- 1 teaspoon mustard
- Croutons and green onions, optional

1. In medium saucepan, melt butter and cook flour over medium heat, stirring constantly, for 3 minutes or until bubbly.

2. Stir in onion soup mix until thoroughly blended with milk and Worcestershire sauce. Bring just to the boiling point, then simmer, stirring occasionally, for 10 minutes.

3. Stir in remaining ingredients and simmer, stirring constantly, for 5 minutes or until cheese is melted.

4. Garnish with additional cheese, croutons, and chopped green onions as desired.

STOUT FRENCH ONION SOUP

Perfect Pairing
Pair this with French Dip Sandwiches on pagev 80.

Ingredients

- **6 medium yellow onions, thinly sliced**
- **3 teaspoons minced garlic**
- **2 tablespoons butter**
- **1 (8 ounce) package baby portobello mushrooms, sliced**
- **6 cups beef broth**
- **½ cup stout**
- **1 tablespoon soy sauce**
- **1 teaspoon red wine vinegar**
- **¼ teaspoon dried rosemary**
- **¼ teaspoon dried thyme**
- **Salt & black pepper, to taste**
- **Sourdough or French bread**
- **6 ounces Irish cheddar cheese, sliced**

1. Pour the sliced onions, garlic, butter, and mushrooms into a big slow cooker. Cover and cook on high for 1 hour or until the onions begin to soften.

2. Add the broth, stout, soy sauce, vinegar, rosemary, thyme, salt, and black pepper and stir to combine. Cover and cook on low for 6 to 8 hours (high, 3 to 4 hours), until the onions are nice and tender.

3. Just before serving, preheat the broiler. Cut the bread into pieces that will fit in your serving bowls and top with the cheese.

4. Broil a minute or two until the cheese is bubbly and slightly browned, watching carefully so it doesn't burn. Ladle the soup into bowls and top with the toasted cheese bread.

SERVES 6

IRISH BEEF STEW

Stout

SERVES 3

Ingredients

- 2 tablespoons olive oil
- 1 ½ pounds stew meat, cut into ½-inch pieces
- 1 onion, chopped
- 1 (12 ounce) bottle stout
- 1¼ cups tomato sauce
- 2 teaspoons fresh rosemary, chopped
- 1 cup frozen peas
- Salt and pepper, to taste

1. Heat olive oil in a saucepan over medium-high heat; add stew meat and onion. Cook for 8 minutes, stirring occasionally.

2. Pour in stout and tomato sauce; bring to a boil. Add rosemary, reduce the heat, cover, and simmer for 2 hours or until the meat is tender.

3. Stir in frozen peas, season with salt and pepper, and ladle into bowls

Perfect Pairing

This stew is perfectly paired with the Spiked Poppy Seed Muffins on page 111.

Bourbon

MAKES 4 CUPS

HAPPY TIMES CORN CHOWDER

Ingredients

- ¼ cup unsalted butter
- 1 onion, diced
- 2 (14.75 ounce) cans creamed corn
- ½ teaspoon ground nutmeg
- 1 to 1 ½ teaspoon salt
- Black pepper, to taste
- Hot sauce
- ½ cup chicken stock
- ½ cup heavy cream
- ¼ cup bourbon
- 8 bacon strips, cooked and diced

Perfect Pairing

Try this with the Beer-Dipped Grilled Cheese on page 79. You'll thank us later.

1. Melt the butter in a saucepan over medium heat. Add the onion and cook for 5 minutes, until it starts to brown, stirring occasionally.

2. Stir in the corn, nutmeg, salt, black pepper, a few dashes of hot sauce, stock, and heavy cream. Let it simmer until it's piping hot, stirring occasionally.

3. Remove the saucepan from the heat and slowly stir in the bourbon. Ladle into mugs and top with a handful of bacon. Unbelievably wonderful!

Bourbon

Perfect Pairing
Serve this with Skillet Bourbon Cornbread on page 62 for extra bourbon deliciousness.

SERVES 6

BOURBON CHILI

Ingredients

- **2 pounds lean ground beef**
- **1 tablespoon olive oil**
- **1 red onion, chopped**
- **2 bell peppers, any color, chopped**
- **1 (28 ounce) can petite diced tomatoes**
- **2½ teaspoons minced garlic**
- **3 to 4 tablespoons chili powder**
- **½ teaspoon cayenne pepper**
- **1 teaspoon paprika**
- **2 to 3 teaspoons ground cumin**
- **Salt and black pepper, to taste**
- **2 ounces dark chocolate**
- **¼ to ½ cup bourbon**
- **Sour cream, shredded cheddar cheese, corn chips, and cooked bacon, for topping**

1. In a large saucepan, brown the ground beef in hot oil over medium heat. After a few minutes, toss in the onion and peppers. Let that cook until the veggies have softened and the meat is cooked through. Drain.

2. Stir in the tomatoes, garlic, chili powder, cayenne, paprika, cumin, salt, and black pepper; bring to a boil, reduce heat, cover, and simmer for 1 hour, stirring occasionally. If you want a thinner chili, stir in some water.

3. Break the chocolate into small pieces and toss it into the chili, stirring until melted. Stir in the bourbon.

4. Top each bowl of chili with sour cream, cheese, chips, and bacon.

LIGHT OPTIONS

Using beer and bourbon in your cooking doesn't necessarily mean you only have to make heavy, beefy dinners. In this section, there are recipes for salad, fish dishes, and quick and easy sandwiches—all infused with that iconic beer and bourbon flavor.

SERVES
6

BEER-BATTERED COD SANDWICHES

Ingredients

- **2 tablespoons olive oil**
- **6 to 8 (6 ounce) cod fillets, patted dry**
- **6 ciabatta or potato rolls**
- **2 tablespoons Old Bay seasoning**
- **1 cup flour**
- **2 teaspoons garlic salt**

- **2 teaspoons black pepper**
- **1 (12 ounce) bottle light lager**
- **1 egg, beaten**
- **Tartar sauce, optional**
- **Coleslaw, optional**

1. Preheat the oven to 275° and set a baking sheet in the oven. Heat oil in a deep fryer to 365°. Meanwhile, cut the fish to fit the rolls.

2. In a bowl, mix Old Bay, flour, garlic salt, and black pepper. In a separate bowl, whisk together the beer and egg; add to the dry ingredients and stir to combine.

3. One or two at a time, dip the fish into the batter, letting the excess drip off, and carefully add to the hot oil. Fry for 5 to 7 minutes, until golden brown on the outside and opaque in the middle.

4. Set the fried fish on the hot baking sheet in the oven to keep warm. Repeat with the remaining fish. Serve on rolls with tartar sauce and coleslaw.

LAGER WATERMELON PUNCH

SERVES 10

Ingredients

- **1 large seedless watermelon**
- **2 tablespoons sugar**
- **1 (12 ounce) can frozen limeade**
- **4 (12 ounce) bottles light lager**
- **8 ounces cherry vodka**

1. Remove and discard the rind of the watermelon and roughly chop the fruit into 2-inch pieces.

2. Place the watermelon in a food processor and pulse until liquefied. Pour through a mesh strainer to remove the pulp. Discard the pulp and repeat the process until the whole watermelon has been blended. You should end up with roughly 6 cups of watermelon juice.

3. Add sugar and frozen limeade to the juice and stir until dissolved. Refrigerate until ready to use.

4. When ready to serve, transfer the juice to a large pitcher. Add light lager and cherry vodka and stir to combine. Serve over ice.

Perfect Pairing

Try these cocktails crafted with complementary alcohol. It's a match made in heaven.

Wheat Ale

SERVES 1

GRAPEFRUIT SHANDY

Ingredients

- **6 ounces ruby red grapefruit juice**
- **6 ounces wheat ale**

In a large glass, combine ingredients and add ice to fill. Garnish with a grapefruit wedge and fresh mint. If you're feeling adventurous, try swapping the grapefruit juice with lemonade or limeade for a refreshing twist.

Light Options **73**

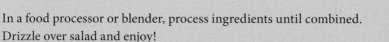

Wheat Ale

BALSAMIC ALE VINAIGRETTE

BACON & ALE PECAN SALAD

Ingredients

- **6 bacon strips, chopped**
- **1 cup packed brown sugar**
- **1 tablespoon salt**
- **1 teaspoon black pepper**
- **⅓ cup wheat ale**
- **1 ½ cups pecan halves**
- **8 cups assorted greens**
- **½ gala apple, cored and thinly sliced**
- **¼ cup blue cheese crumbles**
- **¼ cup red onion, sliced**
- **¼ cup Balsamic Ale Vinaigrette (recipe below)**

SERVES 4

1. Preheat the oven to 350° and grease a rimmed baking sheet with cooking spray.

2. Sauté the bacon until crisp; drain and set aside to cool. In a small saucepan over medium heat, combine the brown sugar, salt, pepper, and wheat ale; let boil for 10 minutes, stirring often.

3. Add the pecans and bacon and stir until coated; spread on the greased baking sheet. Bake for 16 to 18 minutes, turning occasionally. Remove from the oven and allow to cool before breaking apart.

4. For the salad, add the assorted greens to a large bowl and top with apple, blue cheese, red onion, and ½ cup of the toasted bacon and pecan mixture. Add the vinaigrette and toss to coat.

Perfect Pairing

If you're feeling adventurous, top this salad with the Cocktail-Inspired Pecans on page 43 for extra levels of beer and bourbon flavor.

BALSAMIC ALE VINAIGRETTE

Ingredients

- **1 cup wheat ale**
- **1 garlic clove, minced**
- **1 tablespoon honey**
- **1 teaspoon Dijon mustard**

- **1 teaspoon black pepper**
- **⅓ cup olive oil**
- **½ cup balsamic vinegar**

Wheat Ale

MAKES 2 CUPS

In a food processor or blender, process ingredients until combined. Drizzle over salad and enjoy!

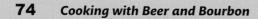

BEER-BOILED SHRIMP

India Pale Ale

MAKES 40–50

Ingredients

- **2 quarts water**
- **2 cups IPA**
- **Juice of 1 lemon**
- **1 tablespoon salt**
- **1 pound medium shrimp**
- **1 tablespoon seafood seasoning**
- **IPA Curry Mayo (recipe below)**

1. In a large pot, bring the water, IPA, lemon juice, and salt to a boil; turn down the heat to a simmer.
2. If needed, devein and peel the shrimp, leaving the tails intact for easy dipping. Add the shrimp and the seafood seasoning to the pot. Cool for a few minutes until the shrimp are opaque, pink, and cooked through.
3. Drain and rinse the shrimp under cold running water to cool. Store covered in the refrigerator until ready to serve.
4. Serve chilled with IPA Curry Mayo.

India Pale Ale

IPA CURRY MAYO

Ingredients

- **1 cup mayo**
- **1 tablespoon curry powder**
- **2 tablespoons IPA**
- **Juice of ½ lime**
- **¼ cup cilantro, chopped**
- **1 teaspoon salt**

Combine ingredients; mix well. Serve with Beer-Boiled Shrimp.

You can tell when a shrimp is done not only by its pink color, but also by its shape. If it looks like a "U" it's undercooked, an "O" means it's overcooked, and a "C" means it's correct.

SERVES
4

SHRIMP & ALE STIR FRY

Ingredients

- 1 tablespoon olive oil
- 1 tablespoon butter
- ½ cup yellow onion, chopped
- ½ to ⅔ cup amber ale
- 2 tablespoons tomato paste
- 2 teaspoons sriracha sauce
- 2 teaspoons honey
- 1 teaspoon brown sugar

- 1 teaspoon soy sauce
- 1 teaspoon sesame seeds
- 1 (12 ounce) package raw shrimp, thawed, peeled, deveined, and patted dry
- 1 ½ cups sugar snap peas
- Fresh cilantro, to taste
- Cooked rice, for serving

1. In a large skillet, heat the oil and butter until melted.

2. Add the onion and cook until soft. Add the amber ale, tomato paste, sriracha sauce, honey, brown sugar, soy sauce, and sesame seeds and bring to a boil.

3. Once boiling, add the shrimp and peas. Cook for 3 minutes; flip and cook another 3 minutes or until the shrimp is pink, cooked through, and curled up. Garnish with fresh cilantro and serve over rice.

BEER-BATTERED FISH & CHIPS

Ingredients

- ¾ cup brown ale
- 2 eggs, separated
- ¾ cup flour
- ¾ teaspoon salt

- 1 ½ teaspoons vegetable oil
- ¼ teaspoon garlic powder
- Shortening
- 25 to 30 pan fish

1. Let brown ale stand at room temperature until it goes flat (about 45 minutes).

2. Beat egg whites until stiff. In a separate bowl, beat the beer, flour, salt, garlic powder, oil, and egg yolks until smooth.

3. Fold in egg whites.

4. Dip in each fillet in the batter separately, and then fry in melted shortening until brown, about 5 to 7 minutes. Turn and brown other side.

5. Serve with Oven Beer Chips (page 78).

Brown Ale

SERVES
12-14

OVEN BEER CHIPS

Ingredients

- 1 ½ pounds russet potatoes
- 1 (12 ounce) bottle brown ale
- 1 tablespoon plus 1 teaspoon sea salt, divided
- Water
- ¼ cup canola oil

- 1 teaspoon garlic powder
- 1 teaspoon onion powder
- 1 teaspoon paprika
- ½ teaspoon black pepper
- ½ teaspoon sugar

1. Cut potatoes into ½-inch-thick slices; cut the slices into large french fry shapes.

2. In a large bowl, mix brown ale and 1 tablespoon sea salt; add the potatoes and enough water to submerge. Cover and chill 3 hours.

3. Position an oven rack in the top ⅓ of the oven and preheat oven to 425°.

4. Drain the potatoes, rinse, pat dry, and put into a clean bowl. Add canola oil, garlic powder, onion powder, paprika, black pepper, sugar, and 1 teaspoon sea salt.

5. Toss to coat the potatoes and spread them out on a rimmed baking sheet. Bake for 20 minutes, flip, and bake 20 minutes longer or until a deep golden brown.

6. Dip in any leftover batter from Beer-Battered Fish and fry to crispy perfection. Serve alongside the fish.

BEER-DIPPED GRILLED CHEESE

Ingredients

- **2 eggs**
- **1 cup brown ale**
- **2 tablespoons flour**
- **½ teaspoon salt**
- **¼ teaspoon chili powder**

- **1 loaf sourdough bread**
- **8 slices sharp cheddar cheese**
- **8 bacon strips, cooked**
- **2 tablespoons butter**

Perfect Pairing

Dip these sandwiches in the Happy Times Corn Chowder on page 69, and witness magic.

1. In a shallow bowl, whisk together eggs, brown ale, flour, salt, and chili powder.

2. Cut the bread into 8 slices, about ½-inch thick. Dunk both sides of one slice into the egg mixture, letting it sit for a few seconds. Lift, let the excess drip back into the bowl, and set the bread slice on a tray.

3. Top with two slices each of sharp cheddar cheese and bacon. Dunk a second slice of bread and set on top. Repeat with the remaining bread, cheese, and bacon.

4. Melt butter in a griddle over medium heat. Set the sandwiches in the hot pan and cook until they're golden brown, then flip them over. When the other side is crispy and golden brown, remove from the heat and serve.

MAKES 4

Brown Ale

SERVES 8

FRENCH DIP SANDWICHES

Ingredients

- 4-pound beef rump roast, trimmed
- 1 (10.5 ounce) can beef broth
- 1 (10.5 ounce) can French onion soup
- 1 (12 ounce) bottle stout
- 1 loaf French bread
- Butter
- Provolone cheese slices

Perfect Pairing

It's like these sandwiches were made to be paired with Stout French Onion Soup on page 68. Give it a try.

1. Preheat the oven to 350°. Set the rump roast into the slow cooker.

2. Add beef broth, French onion soup, and stout to the slow cooker. Cover and cook on low 7 to 8 hours (high, 3½ to 4 hours).

3. Split the French bread lengthwise and spread cut sides with butter; cut into sandwich-size pieces. Bake butter side up 10 to 15 minutes, until heated through and lightly toasted.

4. Meanwhile, cut the meat into thin slices. Pile meat and provolone on the bottoms of the sandwiches; bake a few minutes to melt the cheese. Replace the tops and serve with juice from the slow cooker.

STOUT-GLAZED SALMON & SHROOMS

Ingredients

- 2 pounds white button mushrooms, whole
- 2 shallots, sliced
- 1 teaspoon dried thyme
- 1 cup stout, divided
- 2 tablespoons olive oil
- ½ teaspoon coarse sea salt, divided
- ½ teaspoon black pepper, divided
- 2 tablespoons packed brown sugar
- 1 teaspoon Dijon mustard
- 4 (6 ounce) salmon fillets

SERVES 4

Stout

1. Preheat the oven to 400°.

2. In a large bowl, combine the mushrooms, shallots, thyme, and ¼ cup stout; drizzle with oil, season with ¼ teaspoon each salt and pepper, and toss to combine.

3. Arrange the mushroom mixture in a single layer on a large, rimmed baking sheet. Roast the mushrooms, stirring 2 or 3 times, for 20 minutes. Remove from the oven and set aside.

4. Meanwhile, in a small saucepan, stir together the brown sugar, mustard, and remaining ¾ cup stout and bring the mixture to a boil. Reduce the heat and simmer for 5 to 8 minutes or until the liquid is reduced to about ½ cup. Remove from the heat and set the glaze aside. Reserve half of the glaze for serving.

5. Pat the fish dry and season with the remaining ¼ teaspoon each salt and pepper. Place skin-side down in a large baking dish. Toss the roasted mushrooms with 2 tablespoons of the glaze and arrange them around fish; drizzle with any juice in the pan. Brush the fish with an additional 2 tablespoons of the glaze.

6. Roast until the fish is just cooked through and flakes easily, about 10 to 13 minutes. Serve with the reserved glaze on the side.

STOUT-GLAZED POLLOCK

Ingredients

- 2 (12 ounce) bottles stout
- ⅓ cup honey
- 1 tablespoon lemon juice
- ½ teaspoon hot sauce
- ½ teaspoon salt
- 1 (16 ounce) package frozen pollock fillets, thawed and patted dry
- Olive oil
- Coarse black pepper
- 4 large carrots, cut into ½-inch-thick sticks

1. In a medium skillet, bring the beer and honey to a boil over medium heat; skim foam off the top. Simmer about 45 minutes or until it's reduced to about ¾ cup glaze; transfer to a bowl and stir in lemon juice, hot sauce, and salt. Set aside until cool.

2. Pour ½ cup of the cooled glaze over the fish in a shallow baking dish; turn to coat. Cover and refrigerate several hours. Set the remaining glaze aside.

3. Preheat the broiler. Remove the fish from the marinade and arrange on a greased broiler pan. Brush with oil and season with black pepper. Broil 4 inches from the heat for 4 to 5 minutes or until cooked through.

4. In the meantime, cook the carrots until crisp-tender; serve the carrots with the fish, brushing the fish (and the carrots if you'd like) with the set-aside glaze.

Stout

SERVES
4

IRRESISTIBLE BOURBON SALMON

Bourbon

Ingredients

- ¾ cup bourbon
- ⅔ cup brown sugar
- 1 teaspoon garlic, minced
- 1 teaspoon apple cider vinegar
- 1 tablespoon Worcestershire sauce
- 1 pound salmon, patted dry
- 1 tablespoon coarse sea salt
- 1 ½ teaspoons black pepper

SERVES 4

Perfect Pairing
Bourbon-glazed salmon with Bacon-Beer Green Beans from page 39? Simply irresistible.

1. In a small saucepan, whisk together the bourbon, brown sugar, garlic, vinegar, and Worcestershire sauce, and bring it to a boil over high heat.

2. Reduce the heat and let the glaze simmer about 10 minutes or until it is reduced to about half. Transfer to a little bowl and set it aside for now.

3. Preheat the broiler and line a baking sheet with buttered foil; set aside. Season both sides of salmon with sea salt and black pepper, and set on the prepped pan. Broil 4 inches from the heat for 8 minutes, until cooked through.

4. Immediately brush the salmon with some of the glaze. There are no rules—use as much or as little as you'd like.

Bourbon

BERRY BOURBON LEMONADE

Ingredients

- ¼ cup sugar
- ¼ cup brown sugar
- ½ cup water
- 2 lemons

- 2 cups fresh blueberries
- 12 fresh mint leaves
- 4 ounces bourbon

Perfect Pairing
Try this cocktail crafted with complementary alcohol. It's a match made in heaven.

1. Make a simple syrup by combining both sugars and water in a saucepan; bring to a simmer over medium heat, stirring until the sugars dissolve. Set this syrup aside to cool.

2. Juice the lemons and set the juice aside (you'll need about ½ cup). With a vegetable peeler, peel off thin strips of the lemon rind, avoiding the white pith, and toss into a pitcher along with the blackberries and mint leaves. Stir well.

3. Pour in the bourbon, set-aside lemon juice, and cooled simple syrup; stir to combine.

4. Divide the bourbon mixture among four ice-filled glasses, pouring through a strainer to remove pulp. Garnish with extra blackberries, lemon slices, and mint leaves.

SERVES 4

MEATS & BBQ

You may be used to cracking open a cold one while you're cooking dinner, but these recipes are here to prove that beer can taste just as good in the pan as it is in the can. Turn your attention to the recipes with bourbon as well if you're in the mood to cook something rich, full, and downright delicious.

**SERVES
4**

BEER CAN CHICKEN

Ingredients

- **1 cup butter, divided**
- **2 tablespoons garlic salt, divided**
- **2 tablespoons paprika, divided**
- **Salt and pepper, to taste**
- **1 (12 ounce) can American pale lager**
- **1 (4 pound) whole chicken**

Tip:
Try different types of beer! Stouts and porters add a hint of malt; ales and IPAs, a floral note; wheat, a fruity tone. American lagers add little flavor and primarily keep the meat moist. One opinion: If it's in a can, it's not strong enough. Drink it and add a premium bottle of beer to the can.

1. Preheat an outdoor grill for low heat and lightly oil grate.

2. In a small skillet, melt ½ cup butter. Mix in 1 tablespoon garlic salt, 1 tablespoon paprika, and salt and pepper.

3. Discard half the beer, leaving remainder in the can. Add remaining butter, garlic salt, paprika, and desired amount of salt and pepper to beer can. Place the beer can on a disposable baking sheet.

4. Set the chicken on the can, so the can is in the cavity of the chicken. Baste chicken with the melted, seasoned butter.

5. Place baking sheet with beer and chicken on the prepared grill. Cook over low heat for about 3 hours or until chicken is no longer pink and juices run clear.

BUBBLIN' BEER DOGS

American Pale Lager

Ingredients

- **6 deli-style beef hot dogs**
- **1 (12 ounce) can American pale lager**
- **6 hot dog buns, split**
- **Relish, ketchup, mustard, or your favorite toppings**

In a large saucepan, bring the beer to a boil over high heat. Prick each hot dog several times with a fork; add to the boiling beer and boil for 5 to 6 minutes until heated through. Serve in the buns and top with your favorite hot dog toppings.

MAKES 4

Perfect Pairing
Try piling the Brewer's Beans from page 38 on the top or on the side of your hot dogs.

BRATWURST & BEER

Pilsner

Ingredients

- **2 pounds bratwurst**
- **2 onions, thinly sliced**
- **1 cup butter**
- **6 (12 ounce) cans or bottles pilsner**
- **1 ½ teaspoons ground black pepper**
- **Potato rolls, sauerkraut, mustard, or any other accompaniments you like**

1. Prick bratwurst with fork to prevent them from exploding as they cook, then place them in a large stew pot.

2. Add onions and butter or margarine and slowly pour pilsner into the pot. Place pot over medium heat and simmer for 15 to 20 minutes.

3. Preheat grill for medium-high heat. Lightly oil grate and place bratwurst on grill.

4. Cook for 10 to 14 minutes, turning to brown evenly. Serve hot off the grill with sauerkraut, rolls, or whatever side dish you prefer.

SERVES 8

BEER-BQ PIZZA

Ingredients

- 3 cups all-purpose flour, plus more for dusting
- 1 tablespoon baking powder
- ½ teaspoon salt
- 1 (12 ounce) can pilsner
- 1 tablespoon olive oil
- ½ cup Kickin' Stout BBQ (recipe below)
- 2 cups shredded Gouda cheese
- Red onion, sliced
- Flamin' Beer Jalapeños (recipe on page 28)
- Baby bella mushrooms, sliced, to taste
- Fresh cilantro

SERVES 4

1. Preheat oven to 450°.

2. Combine the flour, baking powder, and salt in a large bowl and mix thoroughly.

3. Pour in the pilsner and mix until combined (the dough will be sticky). Sprinkle the outside of the dough with flour and form a ball. Grease a pizza pan with cooking spray and use a rolling pin to roll the dough into a circle. Roll and crimp the edges of the dough to create a crust; brush the dough with olive oil and poke a few holes with a fork.

4. Bake for 10 minutes and remove from the oven. Top with the Kickin' Stout BBQ, Gouda cheese, red onion, Flamin' Beer Jalapeños, and mushrooms to taste.

5. Bake for an additional 10 minutes or until golden brown on top. Garnish with cilantro.

MAKES 1½ CUPS

KICKIN' STOUT BBQ

Ingredients

- 1 tablespoon olive oil
- 1 teaspoon minced garlic
- ¼ cup soy sauce
- 2 tablespoons tomato paste
- 2 tablespoons ketchup
- 2 tablespoons Worcestershire sauce
- 2 tablespoons apple cider vinegar
- 1 teaspoon chipotle powder
- ½ teaspoon onion powder
- 1 cup stout
- ½ cup packed brown sugar

Heat olive oil in a pan over medium heat and stir in garlic. Add the rest of the ingredients; cook until thickened, stirring occasionally.

SERVES
6

LAGER-MARINATED STEAK TACOS

Ingredients

- **1 (12 ounce) bottle light lager**
- **Juice of 2 limes**
- **2 tablespoons olive oil**
- **1 teaspoon red pepper flakes**
- **½ teaspoon garlic salt**
- **½ teaspoon salt**
- **½ teaspoon black pepper**

- **2 pounds beef flat iron steak**
- **1 red onion, sliced**
- **12 corn tortillas**
- **2 avocados, sliced**
- **¼ cup cilantro, chopped**
- **¼ cup cotija cheese, crumbled**
- **Lime wedges**

1. In a large resealable bag, mix the light lager, lime juice, olive oil, red pepper flakes, garlic salt, salt, and black pepper until combined. Add the steak and onions to the marinade and turn to coat. Refrigerate for at least 30 minutes.

2. Move the oven rack 6 inches from the heating element and preheat the broiler. Preheat a cast-iron grill pan by placing it in the oven for 15 to 20 mins.

3. Pull out the oven rack, lay the steak and onions on the pan, and discard the marinade. Broil for about 4 minutes on each side, or until the steak reaches the desired color and the onions are crisp-tender.

4. Let the steak rest for 5 minutes before cutting diagonally across the grain into thin slices. Serve on corn tortillas with the grilled onions, avocados, cilantro, and cotija cheese. Use the lime wedges for drizzling.

BEER-GARITAS

Ingredients

- **2 (16 ounce) cans light lager**
- **1 cup tequila**
- **1 (12 ounce) can frozen limeade concentrate, thawed**
- **Lime juice**
- **Salt**
- **Lime wedges**

Perfect Pairing

Try this cocktail crafted with complementary alcohol. It's a match made in heaven.

Mix light lager, tequila, and limeade concentrate in a big pitcher. Rim 5 glasses with lime juice and salt, fill glasses with ice, and pour in the margarita mixture. Garnish with lime wedges.

Light Lager

SERVES
5

MAKES
24

SLOW COOKER TACOS

Ingredients

- 1 tablespoon chili powder
- 1 ½ teaspoons ground cumin
- ½ teaspoon smoked paprika
- Pinch of cayenne pepper
- 1 ½ teaspoons salt
- ½ teaspoon black pepper
- 1 (12 ounce) bottle wheat ale

- 3 ½ pounds chicken breast meat
- 1 (16 ounce) jar thick black bean and corn salsa
- Fresh cilantro, chopped, to taste
- 1 onion, chopped
- 1 handful grape tomatoes, diced
- 24 (6-inch) corn tortillas

1. Mix chili powder, cumin, paprika, cayenne, salt, and black pepper; pull out 1½ tablespoons and set it aside. To the remainder, stir in ¾ cup beer.

2. Put the chicken in a greased slow cooker and pour in the spicy beer mixture. Cook on low 6 to 8 hours (high, 3 to 4 hours), until done.

3. Meanwhile, stir together the salsa, cilantro, onion, tomatoes, and as much of the remaining ½ cup of beer as you'd like without thinning the salsa too much; refrigerate until you're ready to use it.

4. When the chicken is done, uncover the cooker, but don't turn it off. Shred the meat and let it soak in the juices about 20 minutes.

5. Meanwhile, fry the tortillas one at a time in hot oil until crisp, folding slightly into a taco shell shape; drain on paper towels.

6. Taste the chicken and stir in more of the set-aside spice mixture if you'd like. Pile the meat, chilled salsa, and your favorite toppings into the shells. They're beer-y, beer-y good!

THE LUMBERJACK

Ingredients

- **2 ounces apple-flavored whiskey**
- **Juice of ¼ lemon**
- **1 ounce pure maple syrup**
- **6 ounces wheat ale**

Mix the apple-flavored whiskey, lemon juice, and maple syrup until combined. Stir in the wheat ale. Add ice to fill the glass and garnish with a twist of lemon peel.

Perfect Pairing
Try this cocktail crafted with complementary alcohol. It's a match made in heaven.

SERVES
1

Wheat Ale

PALE ALE & CHILI-LIME DRUMETTES

Ingredients

- 1 (12 ounce) bottle pale ale
- 3 tablespoons tomato paste
- 3 tablespoons lime juice
- 1 tablespoon chili powder
- ½ teaspoon salt
- ½ teaspoon smoked paprika
- ½ teaspoon garlic powder
- 2 tablespoons honey
- 1 tablespoon soy sauce
- 2 teaspoons hot sauce
- 2 pounds chicken drumettes

Pale Ale

SERVES 4

1. Pour the beer into a large bowl. Whisk in the tomato paste, lime juice, chili powder, salt, paprika, garlic powder, honey, soy sauce, and hot sauce until well blended and smooth. Transfer to a big, zippered plastic bag; add the drumettes, zip to close, turn to coat, and refrigerate for several hours.

2. After the drumettes have marinated several hours, position an oven rack in the top third of the oven and preheat the oven to 400°. Pour the marinade from the bag into a saucepan. Bring to a boil over high heat and cook for 20 minutes or until thickened and reduced, stirring often.

3. Line a rimmed baking sheet with foil and coat with cooking spray. Dip the drumettes into the thickened sauce and arrange them on the baking sheet.

4. Bake for 10 minutes, brush with more sauce, and flip. Repeat every 10 minutes for 40 minutes until cooked through. If you'd like, pop the pan of drumettes under the broiler for a minute or two to crisp up after you take them out of the oven.

Pale Ale

SERVES 4

LEMON SHANDY

Ingredients

- ½ cup lemonade
- ½ cup pale ale

Rim four tall glasses with lemon juice and coarse sugar. Fill the glasses with ice and pour lemonade into each. Top off each glass with pale ale. Garnish with a lemon slice.

Perfect Pairing

Try this cocktail crafted with complementary alcohol. It's a match made in heaven.

MAKES 15–20

IPA SRIRACHA WINGS

Ingredients

- **2 pounds chicken drumettes and wingettes**
- **3½ cups IPA, divided**
- **1 tablespoon salt**
- **¾ cup ketchup**
- **½ cup sriracha sauce**

- **1 tablespoon apple cider vinegar**
- **2 tablespoons soy sauce**
- **1 teaspoon ginger, freshly ground**
- **1 teaspoon Worcestershire sauce**
- **1 tablespoon cornstarch**

1. Combine the chicken drumettes and wingettes, 3 cups IPA, and salt in a plastic container and refrigerate for at least 3 hours.

2. Preheat the oven to 350°. Drain the wings and spread out on a greased rimmed baking sheet.

3. Bake until cooked through, about 35 minutes. If you like your wings extra crispy, broil them for 3 to 4 minutes, until the skin is golden brown and delicious.

4. In a small saucepan, combine the remaining ½ cup IPA with ketchup, sriracha sauce, vinegar, soy sauce, ginger, Worcestershire sauce, and cornstarch. Bring to a simmer.

5. When the wings are done, toss them with the sauce while hot. Serve with ranch dressing for dipping.

IPA PULLED PORK

Ingredients

- 1 ½ teaspoons paprika
- 1 teaspoon onion powder
- 1 teaspoon garlic powder
- 1 teaspoon dried oregano
- 1 teaspoon thyme
- ½ teaspoon black pepper
- 1 teaspoon salt
- 3 ½ pounds boneless pork roast
- 2 tablespoons vegetable oil
- 2 tablespoons butter
- 2 onions, sliced
- 1 (12 ounce) bottle IPA
- ¾ cup Bourbon "Q" Sauce (recipe below)
- Buns, for serving

1. Stir together the paprika, onion powder, garlic powder, oregano, thyme, black pepper, and salt. Rub this mixture evenly over the pork, using your hands.

2. Heat the oil in a skillet over medium-high heat and add the pork, turning to brown all sides. When it's nice and brown, put it in a greased 3-quart slow cooker.

3. Put the butter in the hot skillet and add the onions, a pinch of salt, and half the beer (set the remaining beer aside); cook about 10 minutes, until tender, then dump the onions and the juices over the pork.

4. Mix the Bourbon "Q" Sauce with the set-aside beer and pour it over the onions. Set the cooker to low for 8 hours (high, 4 hours) or until the pork is done.

5. Once the pork is cooked to perfection, pull it out of the cooker and set it on a rimmed baking pan. Shred the meat and serve on buns. You can add cabbage and extra Bourbon "Q" Sauce.

BOURBON "Q" SAUCE

Ingredients

- 1 cup ketchup
- ½ cup bourbon
- 3 tablespoons brown sugar
- 3 tablespoons molasses
- 3 tablespoons apple cider vinegar
- 2 tablespoons Worcestershire sauce
- 1 tablespoon soy sauce
- 1 tablespoon Dijon mustard
- 1½ teaspoons liquid smoke
- 1 teaspoon onion powder
- 1 teaspoon garlic powder
- ½ teaspoon crushed red pepper
- ½ teaspoon black pepper

MAKES
2
CUPS

In a saucepan, combine all ingredients; bring to a boil, stirring occasionally. Reduce heat and simmer until reduced to 2 cups, stirring often. Use in IPA Pulled Pork and anywhere else you please.

India Pale Ale

Note:
Use leftovers for
Bourbon Pulled Pork
Pizza (page 108).

SERVES
4

BEER-DOUSED BURGERS

Ingredients

- **1 tablespoon olive oil**
- **1 tablespoon butter**
- **1 large Vidalia onion, thinly sliced**
- **½ teaspoon minced garlic**
- **1 teaspoon dried thyme**
- **2 pounds ground beef**
- **½ teaspoon salt**
- **½ teaspoon black pepper**
- **1 (12 ounce) bottle brown ale**
- **1 teaspoon balsamic vinegar**
- **1 tablespoon steak sauce**
- **½ teaspoon Dijon mustard**
- **4 slices provolone cheese**

Perfect Pairing

These burgers are elevated with some Beer-Simmered Corn (page 39) on the side.

1. Melt the olive oil and butter in a large skillet over medium heat. Add the onions, garlic, and thyme to the skillet and cook, stirring occasionally, until the onions begin to soften.

2. While the onions are cooking, season the ground beef with salt and pepper and form it into four patties. Push the softened onions to the outer edge of the skillet and add the burgers to the skillet. Cook the burgers for 2 to 3 minutes and then flip over. Add the brown ale, vinegar, steak sauce, and mustard to the pan and gently stir to combine.

3. Continue cooking the burgers to your desired color. Remove burgers from the skillet and continue to reduce the remaining liquid until it reaches a gravy-like consistency.

4. Serve the burgers on buns and top each with caramelized onions, provolone cheese, and the brown ale reduction.

ROSEMARY BEER CHICKEN

Ingredients

- 1 tablespoon dried rosemary
- 1 teaspoon dried sage
- 3 tablespoons olive oil
- 1 tablespoon honey mustard
- 1 tablespoon honey
- ½ teaspoon salt
- ½ teaspoon black pepper
- 1 teaspoon minced garlic
- 1 (12 ounce) bottle brown ale
- 2 pounds chicken drumsticks

Brown Ale

SERVES 4–5

1. Whisk together the rosemary, sage, olive oil, honey mustard, honey, salt, pepper, garlic, and brown ale in a large bowl or baking dish. Add the chicken and turn to coat; cover and refrigerate for at least 1 hour.

2. Preheat the oven to 375°.

3. Spread the chicken on a foil-lined rimmed baking sheet. Bake at 375° for 45 minutes until the chicken is cooked through and the skin is crispy. Yum!

Perfect Pairing

The only thing that could make this chicken more delicious would be some Sweet Potato Ale Fries (found on page 41).

Wheat Ale

PEACH MOON

Ingredients

- ½ (12 ounce) bottle wheat ale (like Blue Moon)
- 1½ ounces (3 tablespoons) peach schnapps
- ⅓ cup orange juice

Pour half of the beer into a tall glass. Add peach schnapps and orange juice. Fill the glass with the rest of the beer and stir gently (don't get overzealous or the foam will explode out of the glass—seriously). Garnish with an orange slice.

SERVES 2

Perfect Pairing

Try this cocktail crafted with complementary alcohol. It's a match made in heaven.

Serve alongside roasted vegetables, or with mashed potatoes, as shown here

MAKES
6
CHOPS

LAMB CHOPS BRAISED IN BEER

Serve alongside roasted vegetables, or with mashed potatoes, as shown here.

Ingredients

- **6 (1½-inch) lamb rib chops**
- **Salt and pepper, to taste**
- **3 to 4 tablespoons flour**
- **3 tablespoons oil**
- **3 large onions, sliced**

- **6 potatoes, sliced**
- **1 teaspoon thyme**
- **1 can brown ale (enough to show itself under the onions and potatoes)**

1. Salt and pepper lamb chops and coat with flour.

2. Heat the oil and trimmed fat in a skillet with a lid and sauté the chops swiftly on both sides, 2 minutes for each side.

3. Cover the lamb chops with alternating layers of onions and potatoes, each salted and peppered with a bit of thyme.

4. Add the brown ale, cover, and simmer for about 30 minutes over medium heat.

PROSCIUTTO & PORTER FETTUCINE

Porter

Ingredients

- 3 tablespoons olive oil
- 3 ounces prosciutto
- 1 shallot, thinly sliced
- 1 pound baby bella mushrooms, thinly sliced
- 1 teaspoon minced garlic
- 1 teaspoon dried thyme
- ⅓ cup porter
- ½ cup chicken broth
- ⅓ cup heavy cream
- ½ teaspoon salt
- ½ teaspoon black pepper
- 12 ounces fettucine pasta
- ¼ cup freshly grated parmesan

SERVES
4

1. Heat the olive oil in a large skillet over medium-high heat. Add the slices of prosciutto, cooking until crispy. Remove prosciutto from skillet; drain and set aside to cool.

2. Reduce heat to medium; add the shallot and cook until softened. Add the mushrooms, garlic, and thyme and cook until the mushrooms have browned, about 10 minutes.

3. Pour in the porter, scraping to deglaze the bottom of the pan. Stir in the chicken broth, lower the heat, and simmer until the sauce thickens slightly. Stir in the cream, salt, and pepper.

4. Cook the pasta in boiling, salted water until nearly al dente.

5. Drain the pasta and add it to the sauce. Toss to coat.

6. Transfer the pasta to a serving bowl. Top with crumbled prosciutto and grated parmesan.

CHICKEN BEER-SALA

Ingredients

- ¾ cup flour
- 1 teaspoon salt
- 1 teaspoon black pepper
- 4 boneless, skinless chicken breasts
- 2 tablespoons butter
- 1 tablespoon olive oil
- 1 ½ cups white button mushrooms, thinly sliced
- ⅓ cup red onion, thinly sliced
- 1 teaspoon minced garlic
- 1 teaspoon dried thyme
- 1 (12 ounce) bottle porter
- 1 ½ cups chicken stock
- ½ cup shredded mozzarella cheese

1. In a shallow dish, mix the flour, salt, and pepper until combined. Coat both sides of each chicken breast in the flour mixture and shake off any excess.

2. Melt the butter and olive oil in a large skillet over medium-high heat. Brown both sides of the chicken breasts in the hot oil for 2 to 3 minutes; set aside while you make the sauce.

3. Add the mushrooms and onion to the same skillet; sauté for 2 to 3 minutes. Add the garlic and thyme and sauté for 1 minute more.

4. Pour the porter over the mushrooms and gently scrape the brown bits from the pan. Reduce the sauce about 3 minutes and add the chicken stock.

5. Reduce for another 6 to 7 minutes and return the chicken to the pan. Lower the heat to medium and simmer until the chicken is cooked through, about 12 minutes. Sprinkle with mozzarella and let melt before removing the chicken from the skillet.

Porter

SERVES
4

Perfect Pairing
Pair this with Ale-Glazed Carrots & Walnuts on page 41 for a delicious, beer-y, flavorful meal.

BREW-SCHETTA PULLED PORK

Porter

SERVES 4–5

Ingredients

- 1½ to 2 pounds pork tenderloin
- 1 (12 ounce) bottle porter
- ⅓ cup balsamic vinegar
- 1 teaspoon dried basil
- 1 teaspoon salt
- 1 teaspoon black pepper
- ½ teaspoon garlic powder
- ½ teaspoon dried oregano
- ½ teaspoon dried thyme
- ¼ cup brown sugar
- Ciabatta rolls, red onion, tomato, fresh mozzarella, and fresh basil, for serving

1. Place the pork tenderloin into a slow cooker.

2. Whisk together porter, balsamic vinegar, dried basil, salt, black pepper, garlic powder, oregano, thyme, and brown sugar and pour the mixture over the tenderloin.

3. Cook on low for 6 to 7 hours or until the meat is cooked through and easily pulls apart.

4. Shred the meat and serve on ciabatta rolls with red onion, tomato, mozzarella, and basil.

BEER-MARINATED STEAK

Ingredients

- 6 (12 ounce) New York strip steaks
- 1 (12 ounce) bottle porter
- ½ cup brown sugar
- 6 tablespoons lime juice
- 4 to 6 cloves garlic, chopped
- 3 tablespoons Worcestershire sauce
- 4 tablespoons olive oil
- 1 teaspoon hot pepper sauce
- 3 tablespoons whole grain mustard

1. Place steaks in single layer in a glass baking dish.

2. Whisk porter, sugar, lime juice, garlic, Worcestershire sauce, olive oil, hot pepper sauce, and mustard in large bowl to blend. Pour marinade over steaks in baking dish.

3. Cover tightly with plastic wrap and refrigerate overnight.

4. Remove steaks from marinade and grill to desired doneness.

Porter

SERVES 6

Cheesy Beer Mashed Potatoes (page 37)

Porter

Perfect Pairing
Cheesy Beer Mashed Potatoes (page 37) are especially delicious when served alongside this dish.

SERVES 6–8

PORTER POT ROAST

Serve with the roasted veggies or with carrots and mashed potatoes, as seen here.

Ingredients

- 2 tablespoons vegetable oil
- 2 pounds top round steak, trimmed
- 1 onion, chopped
- 2 celery stalks, chopped
- 1 clove garlic, minced
- 1 (10.75 ounce) can condensed cream of mushroom soup
- 1 (12 ounce) can or bottle porter
- 2 bay leaves
- 2 whole cloves

1. Heat a roasting pan over high heat and coat bottom with oil. Sear meat on all sides. Remove from pan and set aside.

2. Reduce heat to low and sauté onion, celery, and garlic, scraping up browned bits. Cover and cook on low for 15 minutes.

3. Mix in cream of mushroom soup and porter. Wrap bay leaves and cloves in cheesecloth, tie with string, and add to pan.

4. Place roast on top of vegetables, spooning some sauce over meat. Cover with foil and place lid over foil to seal well. Reduce heat and simmer for 1½ hours.

5. Remove meat from pan and slice, then return it to the pan and spoon sauce over it. Cook an additional 15 minutes.

TERIYAKI STOUT BEEF

Ingredients

- ½ teaspoon freshly grated ginger
- 1 teaspoon Dijon mustard
- ¼ teaspoon red pepper flakes
- 1 teaspoon sriracha sauce
- 1 teaspoon minced garlic
- ¼ cup honey
- 1 tablespoon brown sugar
- ½ teaspoon black pepper
- 1 pound flat iron steak
- 1 teaspoon salt
- ¼ cup cornstarch
- ¼ cup stout
- 3 tablespoons soy sauce
- 2 tablespoons sesame oil
- 2 tablespoons sesame seeds
- 2 tablespoons green onions, chopped
- Cooked rice, for serving

1. In a small bowl, stir together the ginger, mustard, red pepper flakes, sriracha sauce, garlic, honey, brown sugar, and black pepper; set aside. Thinly slice the steak against the grain and sprinkle with salt.

2. Place the cornstarch in a small bowl and stir together the stout and soy sauce in a separate bowl.

3. Heat the sesame oil in a large skillet over medium heat.

4. A few at a time, dredge the beef strips in the cornstarch, dip into the beer mixture, and add to the skillet. Repeat with all the beef.

5. Once the beef has started to brown, add the honey mixture as well as any of the remaining beer mixture to the skillet. Cook until sauce has thickened.

6. Top with sesame seeds and green onions and serve over rice.

Stout

SERVES
4

MAKES 8

BEER & BOURBON KEBABS

Ingredients

- ½ cup stout
- ¼ cup bourbon
- ¼ cup soy sauce
- 2 tablespoons coarse grain mustard
- 3 tablespoons brown sugar
- ½ teaspoon salt
- 2 tablespoons coarse black pepper
- ½ teaspoon Worcestershire sauce

- ¼ cup green onions, minced
- 1 pound chicken breast meat, cut into 1-inch chunks
- 1 (8 ounce) package whole mushrooms
- 2 bell peppers, any color, cut into 1-inch chunks
- Cooked rice, for serving

1. Combine the beer, bourbon, soy sauce, mustard, sugar, salt, black pepper, Worcestershire sauce, and green onions in a big, zippered plastic bag; zip to close and rub between your hands to blend ingredients. Add the chicken, zip closed, and chill for several hours, turning occasionally.

2. Preheat the oven to 450° and place the oven rack in the top position. Line a baking sheet with foil and coat the foil with cooking spray.

3. Thread the mushrooms, chicken, bell peppers, and onions onto metal skewers. Set the skewers on the prepped baking sheet and brush with some of the marinade; bake for 15 minutes or until the chicken is done.

4. Keeping in mind that the skewers are now scorching hot, grab them using an oven mitt and put on plates with rice. Serve hot.

BOURBON STREET CHICKEN

Ingredients

- 2 tablespoons cornstarch
- 2 tablespoons olive oil
- 2 teaspoons minced garlic
- ¼ teaspoon ground ginger
- ¼ teaspoon salt
- ¼ teaspoon cayenne pepper
- 2 tablespoons applesauce
- ¼ cup bourbon
- ⅓ cup brown sugar
- 2 tablespoons ketchup

- 1 tablespoon apple cider vinegar
- ½ cup water
- ⅓ cup soy sauce
- 3 pounds chicken breast meat, cut into bite-sized pieces
- 4 bacon strips, cooked and crumbled
- Cooked rice, for serving
- 1 fresh pineapple, peeled and cut into bite-sized pieces, for topping

Perfect Pairing
Looking for the perfect side? Look no further than Bourbon Mac & Cheese (page 44).

1. In a 3-quart slow cooker, combine the cornstarch, oil, garlic, ginger, salt, cayenne, applesauce, bourbon, brown sugar, ketchup, vinegar, water, and soy sauce; whisk together until nicely blended.

2. Toss the chicken pieces into the cooker, add the bacon, and give it a good stir, coating the chicken pieces evenly.

3. Cover the cooker, set it to low, let cook for 4 hours or until the chicken is done.

4. Put rice on serving plates, top with the chicken and sauce from the cooker, and top with pineapple pieces.

Bourbon

SERVES
12

CHOPS WITH MUSHROOM-BOURBON CREAM

Ingredients

- **5 tablespoons grapeseed oil, divided**
- **1 pound white mushrooms, sliced**
- **¼ cup onion, chopped**
- **2 garlic cloves, chopped**
- **½ cup dry white wine**
- **1 cup chicken stock**
- **¼ cup plus 2 tablespoons bourbon, divided**

- **½ cup heavy cream**
- **⅓ cup flour**
- **1 egg**
- **1½ cups fresh breadcrumbs**
- **4 (6 to 7 ounce) center-cut pork chops**
- **Salt and black pepper, to taste**
- **2 tablespoons fresh basil, finely chopped**

1. Heat 2 tablespoons oil in a big skillet over medium-high heat and add the mushrooms, onion, and garlic; sauté 10 minutes or until the mushrooms have browned. Add the wine and bring to a boil; boil several minutes, until the liquid is reduced to a glaze-like consistency.

2. Add the stock and ¼ cup bourbon and boil until reduced by about two-thirds. Stir in the cream and simmer until the sauce thickens. Set aside.

3. Put flour into a shallow bowl. In a separate shallow bowl, whisk the egg with the remaining 2 tablespoons bourbon, and put the breadcrumbs into yet another bowl. Sprinkle both sides of the pork with salt and black pepper; dip into the flour, then the egg, and then the breadcrumbs so the chops are completely coated.

4. Heat the remaining 3 tablespoons oil in a separate big skillet over medium-high heat. Add the coated chops and fry 4 minutes per side, until browned. Flip the chops again, reduce the heat to low, cover, and cook for 5 minutes or until done.

5. Reheat the bourbon cream, stir in the basil and more salt and pepper, and serve the chops with the sauce for flavor.

Bourbon & Light Lager

HOP, SKIP & A CUP

Ingredients

- **1 ounce (2 tablespoons) bourbon**
- **1½ tablespoon fresh lemon juice**
- **1½ tablespoon grenadine syrup**
- **6 to 8 ounces light lager, chilled**

Perfect Pairing

Try this cocktail crafted with complementary alcohol. It's a match made in heaven.

In a shaker, combine bourbon, lemon juice, and grenadine; shake vigorously. Pour into a tall glass filled with ice and fill to the top with light lager.

SERVES 1

Bourbon

BOURBON PULLED PORK PIZZA

Ingredients

- **4 to 5 cups of meat and onions from IPA Pulled Pork (recipe on page 94)**
- **1 (12-inch) precooked pizza crust**
- **1 tablespoon olive oil**
- **1 tablespoon bourbon**
- **Bourbon "Q" Sauce (recipe on page 94)**
- **Mushrooms, to taste**
- **Jalapeños, to taste**
- **Pepper Jack cheese**

SERVES 4

1. Preheat the oven to 400° and preheat a pizza pan. While the oven is heating, warm the meat and onions from IPA Pulled Pork.

2. Set the precooked pizza crust on the hot pan and brush olive oil and bourbon over the top of the entire crust; spread with some Bourbon "Q" Sauce to within ½ inch of the edge and top with the warm pork and onions.

3. Add mushrooms and jalapeños or any other toppings to taste. Cover with as much shredded Pepper Jack cheese as you'd like.

4. Bake 10 to 15 minutes or until the cheese is melted. Serve with extra Bourbon "Q" Sauce.

BOURBON PEACH SLUSH

Ingredients

- **1 (16 ounce) package frozen peaches**
- **1 cup ginger ale, chilled**
- **4 ounces (½ cup) bourbon**
- **2 tablespoons sugar**
- **Juice of 1 lime**

Perfect Pairing

Try this cocktail crafted with complementary alcohol. It's a match made in heaven.

Pour the frozen peaches into a blender along with ginger ale, bourbon, sugar, and lime juice. Process until relatively smooth. Pour into two big glasses and enjoy

MAKES 2

DOUSED & SOUSED WINGS

Bourbon

SERVES 4

Ingredients

- **2 ½ pounds chicken wings**
- **3 to 4 tablespoons Dijon mustard**
- **2 cups bourbon**
- **2 tablespoons Angostura bitters**
- **¾ cup sugar**

1. Put chicken wings in a big, zippered plastic bag. Whisk together Dijon mustard, bourbon, bitters, and sugar and pour into the bag with the wings. Zip to close and put in fridge for several hours or overnight to marinate.

2. When you're ready to bake the wings, preheat the oven to 400°. Arrange the wings on a foil-lined and greased rimmed baking sheet and pour the marinade into a saucepan.

3. Bake the wings for 35 to 40 minutes or until cooked through, brushing with marinade a couple of times during baking.

4. In the meantime, boil the marinade until reduced by half. Serve the sauce with the wings and get out the napkins!

FREEZER SLUSH

Bourbon

MAKES ABOUT 12 CUPS

Ingredients

- **5 ½ cups water**
- **3 ½ cups pineapple juice**
- **1 cup sugar**
- **1 (12 ounce) can frozen lemonade concentrate**
- **½ (12 ounce) can frozen orange juice concentrate**
- **2 teaspoons instant tea mix**
- **8 ounces bourbon**
- **Lemon-lime soda, optional**

1. In a freezer container, mix water, pineapple juice, sugar, frozen lemonade and orange juice concentrates, instant tea mix, and bourbon. Stir, cover, and freeze.

2. Take the mixture straight from the freezer and shave into a glass, or thaw in the refrigerator.

3. Add lemon-lime soda if you prefer your slushy to be fizzier.

SWEETS

By now you know that beer and bourbon are excellent ingredients to make your dishes more flavorful and packed with texture and warmth. In these sweet recipes, though, you'll see a whole other side to using them in the kitchen. Remember that beer and bourbon will change the structure of your sweet treats, but will ultimately enhance the taste. For example, beer helps with baked goods' levity and bourbon adds a smoky vanilla flavor to your treats. Yum, yum, and yum again.

MAKES
12

SPIKED POPPY SEED MUFFINS

Ingredients

- **2 ½ cups flour**
- **1 ¾ teaspoons baking powder**
- **¼ teaspoon baking soda**
- **1 teaspoon coarse salt**
- **2 eggs, room temperature**
- **1 cup plus 2 ½ tablespoons sugar, divided**
- **Juice of 2 lemons, divided**
- **¼ cup plus ⅓ cup Boston lager, room temperature**
- **½ cup unsalted butter, melted and cooled**
- **2 to 3 tablespoons poppy seeds**
- **Coarse sugar for sprinkling, optional**
- **Powdered sugar**

Perfect Pairing
Serve this with Irish Beef Stew on page 69 for the perfect pairing of savory and sweet.

1. Preheat the oven to 350°. Grease 12 muffin cups and set aside.

2. In a large bowl, mix the flour, baking powder, baking soda, and salt.

3. In a separate bowl, whisk together the eggs, 1 cup sugar, 1 ½ teaspoons zest, and ¼ cup each lemon juice and beer.

4. Whisk in the butter until blended, then stir this mixture into the dry ingredients until just combined.

5. Stir in the poppy seeds and divide evenly among the prepped muffin cups; sprinkle with coarse sugar for extra texture if you'd like. Bake 18 to 20 minutes, until muffins test done. Set the pan on a cooling rack for 5 minutes before removing the muffins.

6. In the meantime, whisk together the remaining ⅓ cup beer, 2 ½ tablespoons sugar, and 1 teaspoon lemon juice.

7. With a toothpick or skewer, pierce the top of each warm muffin several times and slowly pour some of the beer mixture over each one, letting it soak leisurely into the holes.

8. Whisk together about 1 tablespoon lemon juice with enough powdered sugar to make a drizzling consistency. Drizzle over muffins and sprinkle with more zest.

**SERVES
8–10**

BREWS-KEY LIME PIE

Ingredients

- **2 sleeves graham crackers**
- **½ cup unsalted butter, melted**
- **2 teaspoons plus 1 cup sugar, divided**
- **3 (8 ounce) packages cream cheese, softened**
- **1 cup lime-flavored lager**
- **2 tablespoons lime juice**
- **3 eggs**
- **Whipped cream and lime zest, for topping**

1. Preheat oven to 350°. Mix the graham crackers, butter, and 2 teaspoons sugar in a food processor until crumbled and fully combined.

2. Clean out the food processor and add the cream cheese, lime-flavored lager, lime juice, eggs, and the remaining 1 cup sugar. Blend the filling ingredients until fully mixed and smooth.

3. Grease a 9-inch springform pan and line the bottom with parchment paper. Pour the graham cracker mixture into the pan and press into the bottom and up the sides of the pan. Bake for 10 minutes. Remove from the oven and pour the filling into the pan.

4. Bake for 1 hour. Turn off the oven and open the door for 5 minutes. Close the oven door and let the pie set for 30 minutes inside the oven.

5. Remove the pie from the oven and let it cool completely before removing the springform pan. Serve with whipped cream and lime zest.

SHIRLEY'S SECRET

Ingredients

- **1 ounce grenadine**
- **2 ounces lemonade**
- **6 ounces light lager**

In a highball glass filled with ice, gently stir to combine ingredients. Garnish with a maraschino cherry and a slice of lemon. You'll love this grown-up twist on a Shirley Temple!

Light Lager

SERVES 1

Perfect Pairing
Try this cocktail crafted with complementary alcohol. It's a match made in heaven.

MAKES
6

BUTTERMILK BEER PANCAKES

Ingredients

- 1½ cups brown sugar
- ½ cup light lager
- 3 tablespoons butter
- 1 teaspoon cinnamon, divided
- 2 eggs, room temperature

- ½ teaspoon cream of tartar
- ½ cup wheat ale
- ¼ cup buttermilk
- 1 teaspoon vanilla
- 1 tablespoon orange zest

- 1 cup flour
- 3 tablespoons sugar
- 1 teaspoon baking powder
- ½ teaspoon baking soda
- ½ teaspoon salt

1. For the syrup, put the brown sugar, light beer, butter, and ½ teaspoon cinnamon in a small saucepan over medium-low heat until it just begins to boil, stirring to dissolve; keep warm.

2. For the pancakes, separate the egg whites and yolks into two bowls. Add the cream of tartar to the whites and beat on high speed until stiff peaks form.

3. To the yolks, add the wheat ale, buttermilk, vanilla, and zest, and beat until well mixed.

4. In a large bowl, stir together the flour, sugar, baking powder, baking soda, salt, and the remaining ½ teaspoon cinnamon. Add the yolk mixture to the dry ingredients and stir until combined. Gently fold in the egg whites until batter is blended.

5. Using about ½ cup for each pancake, pour batter onto a hot nonstick griddle or skillet. Cook until bubbles form around the edges; flip and cook until golden brown on the other side. Serve with butter and warm syrup.

WHEAT ALE WAFFLES

Wheat Ale

Ingredients

- **2 cups flour**
- **1 teaspoon baking powder**
- **½ teaspoon baking soda**
- **¼ teaspoon salt**
- **2 tablespoons sugar**
- **2 large eggs, lightly beaten**
- **1 cup wheat ale**
- **¾ cup milk**
- **¼ cup butter, melted**
- **½ teaspoon vanilla extract**
- **1 teaspoon orange zest, plus more for garnish**
- **Powdered sugar, whipped cream, and maple syrup, for topping**

SERVES 5

1. Preheat waffle iron according to manufacturer directions.

2. In a large bowl, whisk together the flour, baking powder, baking soda, salt, and sugar; set aside.

3. In a separate bowl, combine the eggs, wheat ale, milk, butter, vanilla extract, and orange zest. Add the egg mixture to the flour mixture and fold together until just combined. Cook the waffles according to manufacturer directions.

4. Serve warm, topped with powdered sugar, whipped cream, maple syrup, and orange zest.

Beer in waffles . . . who would've guessed? Belgian-style wheat ales are flavored with orange peel, coriander, and other subtle spice notes. This makes them a great addition to citrusy recipes and desserts.

Light Lager

BRUNCH PUNCH

Ingredients

- **4 ounces orange juice**
- **6 ounces light lager**
- **1 ounce amaretto**

Perfect Pairing

Try this cocktail crafted with complementary alcohol. It's a match made in heaven.

Add ingredients to a pint glass. Stir together and add enough ice to fill the glass. Garnish with an orange slice. No need to feel guilty, the orange juice makes this cocktail part of a well-balanced breakfast.

SERVES 1

MAKES
24

CITRUS ALE CUPCAKES

Ingredients

- **¼ cup milk**
- **1 (12 ounce) bottle wheat ale, divided**
- **2 ½ cups all-purpose flour**
- **2 teaspoons baking powder**
- **½ teaspoon salt**
- **¾ cup plus 6 tablespoons unsalted butter, divided**
- **1 ¾ cups sugar**
- **3 eggs**
- **1 teaspoon vanilla extract**
- **1 ½ teaspoons orange zest, divided**
- **12 ounces cream cheese, softened**
- **1 tablespoon orange juice**
- **4 cups powdered sugar**
- **Orange wedges**

1. Preheat the oven to 375° and line 24 standard muffin cups with liners.

2. In a small bowl, combine the milk and 1 cup wheat ale.

3. In a large mixing bowl, whisk together flour, baking powder, and salt and set aside. With an electric mixer, beat together ¾ cup butter and the sugar for 2 to 3 minutes or until fluffy.

4. Add the eggs one at a time, beating well after each addition. Mix in the vanilla extract and ½ teaspoon orange zest. Alternately add the dry and wet ingredients to the butter mixture with the mixer on low, beginning and ending with the dry ingredients.

5. Fill each liner ⅔ full and bake for 18 minutes, or until a toothpick comes out clean. While they are still warm, poke holes in the top of each cupcake with a toothpick and brush the remainder of the beer on top.

6. For the frosting, mix the cream cheese and the remaining 6 tablespoons butter with an electric mixer. Beat in the orange juice and 1 teaspoon orange zest. Gradually add the powdered sugar, beating until smooth.

7. Using a piping bag fitted with a star tip, pipe the frosting onto cold cupcakes. Garnish with orange wedges and zest.

SPIKED CITRUS SANGRIA

Ingredients

- 1 grapefruit
- 1 navel orange
- 1 lime
- 1 lemon

- 16 ounces pineapple juice
- 8 ounces vodka
- 3 (12 ounce) bottles wheat ale

1. Wash and thinly slice the fruit.

2. Combine the sliced fruit, pineapple juice, and vodka in a large pitcher. Refrigerate for at least 2 hours.

3. When you're ready to serve, add the wheat ale to the fruit mixture. Serve over ice.

Perfect Pairing

Try this cocktail crafted with complementary alcohol. It's a match made in heaven.

SERVES 8

Wheat Ale

MAKES 9

HOPPED-UP LEMON BARS

Ingredients

- **1¼ cups flour, divided**
- **⅓ cup powdered sugar, plus more for dusting**
- **6 tablespoons unsalted butter**
- **¼ teaspoon salt**
- **3 eggs**

- **1½ cups sugar**
- **2 tablespoons cornstarch**
- **¼ cup freshly squeezed lemon juice**
- **⅓ cup IPA**
- **1 teaspoon lemon zest**

1. Preheat oven to 350°.

2. Add 1 cup flour, powdered sugar, butter, and salt to a food processor. Process until well combined. Press into the bottom of a greased 8″ x 8″ pan. Chill for 15 minutes.

3. Bake the crust for 20 to 25 minutes or until golden brown. Remove from the oven and cool to room temperature.

4. In a large bowl, whisk together the eggs, sugar, the remaining ¼ cup flour, and cornstarch. Add the lemon juice, IPA, and zest; stir until combined. Pour the filling over the cooled crust. Bake at 350 ° until the center has set, about 25 to 30 minutes.

5. Allow to cool slightly before refrigerating. Chill for 2 to 3 hours before cutting. Dust with powdered sugar before serving.

RASPBERRY BLISS

Ingredients

- ¼ cup fresh raspberries
- 2 teaspoons sugar
- ½ ounce vodka
- 6 ounces IPA

1. In a large cocktail glass, mix raspberries and sugar.
2. Add vodka and stir to combine; top with IPA and add ice to fill.
3. Garnish with a fresh raspberry. Now that's a refreshing cocktail!

India Pale Ale

SERVES
1

MAKES 12

RASPBERRY ALE SHORTCAKE

Ingredients

- **4 cups biscuit baking mix**
- **1½ cups sugar**
- **1 tablespoon lemon juice**

- **1 (12 ounce) bottle amber ale, plus 1 cup**
- **2 cups fresh raspberries**
- **Whipped cream, for topping**

1. Preheat the oven to 400°.

2. Mix biscuit baking mix, ½ cup sugar, lemon juice, and 1 bottle amber ale.

3. Pour into 12 greased muffin tins. Bake for 15 to 20 minutes, or until a toothpick comes out clean.

4. For the sauce, combine raspberries, 1 cup sugar, and 1 cup amber ale in a saucepan over medium-high heat.

5. Allow to simmer, stirring occasionally, until reduced and thickened, about 20 minutes.

6. Spoon the sauce over the shortcakes, top with whipped cream, and enjoy!

PUB CARAMEL CORN

Ingredients

- 2 (3.5 ounce) bags microwavable popcorn, popped
- 1 cup chopped pecans
- 1 cup pretzels, crushed
- 1 (12 ounce) bottle brown ale
- 3 tablespoons unsalted butter

- 2 cups brown sugar
- 1 cup heavy cream
- ¼ teaspoon salt
- 2 teaspoons vanilla extract
- ½ teaspoon baking soda

1. Preheat oven to 250°.

2. Spread the popped popcorn, pecans, and pretzels on a large, foil-lined rimmed baking sheet; place in the oven to keep warm.

3. Add the brown ale and butter to a saucepan and bring to a low boil. Add the brown sugar and boil until it looks like thick syrup; stir in the cream until combined. Continue to cook for about 5 minutes or until caramel thickens.

4. Remove from the heat and add the salt, vanilla extract, and baking soda. Remove the popcorn mixture from the oven and add the caramel; mix until everything is well coated.

5. Return to the oven and bake for 1 hour, stirring every 15 minutes.

6. Spread the caramel corn mixture on parchment paper to cool. Store in an airtight container.

Brown Ale

MAKES
12
CUPS

Chocolate Porter

CHOCOLATE PORTER PIE

Ingredients

- 1 (4 ounce) package semisweet baking chocolate
- 2½ tablespoons plus ¼ cup chocolate porter, divided
- 1½ tablespoons plus 3¾ cups heavy cream, divided
- 1 (9-inch) chocolate pie crust, purchased
- 1 (4 ounce) package unsweetened baking chocolate
- 1¼ cups powdered sugar, divided
- 8 ounces mascarpone cheese, softened
- 1 teaspoon vanilla

SERVES 8

1. Chop the semisweet chocolate and toss into a small bowl. Microwave 2 ½ tablespoons porter with 1 ½ tablespoons cream until it's just starting to steam; pour over the chocolate, let stand to soften, and stir until melted. Pour into the crust and chill for 30 minutes.

2. Chop the unsweetened chocolate and put into the same bowl. Combine ¼ cup cream and the remaining ¼ cup beer and microwave until steaming; pour over the chocolate, let stand to soften, and stir until melted. Let sit to cool to room temperature.

3. In a chilled mixing bowl, beat 1 ½ cups cream with ½ cup powdered sugar on high speed until soft peaks form. With the mixer running, slowly add the cooled chocolate mixture, beating until stiff peaks form; spread over the chocolate layer in the pie plate. Chill until set.

4. The rest of the porter? You get to drink it.

5. Beat the mascarpone and remaining ¾ cup powdered sugar. Add the vanilla and remaining 2 cups cream, beating until medium peaks form. Mound on top of the pie and chill.

TAVERN COOKIES

Stout

Ingredients

- 1 (12 ounce) bottle stout
- ¾ cup unsalted butter, cubed
- ⅔ cup packed brown sugar
- ½ cup sugar
- 1 egg, plus 1 yolk
- 1 teaspoon vanilla extract
- 1 cup all-purpose flour
- ¾ cup bread flour
- 1 teaspoon cornstarch
- ½ teaspoon baking soda
- ¼ teaspoon salt
- 1 cup dark chocolate chips
- ½ cup broken pretzels
- ¼ cup dry-roasted peanuts

MAKES 24

1. Add the stout to a pot over medium heat and simmer, stirring occasionally, until reduced to about 2 tablespoons of liquid, about 15 to 20 minutes.

2. In the bowl of a stand mixer, add the butter and both types of sugar; beat together until creamed. Add the egg and the yolk and mix until well combined. Add the stout reduction and vanilla extract and beat until combined, scraping the bottom to make sure all the ingredients are mixed.

3. In a separate bowl, whisk together both types of flour, cornstarch, baking soda, and salt. Add the dry ingredients to the stand mixer bowl and mix on medium speed until just barely combined. Add the chocolate chips, pretzels, and peanuts and stir to incorporate.

4. Cover a rimmed baking sheet with parchment paper; scoop the dough and roll into golf ball-sized rounds. Place on the baking sheet, cover with plastic wrap, and chill for at least 3 hours.

5. Preheat the oven to 350°. Bake for 16 to 21 minutes or until golden brown.

Stout

SHORT & STOUT

Ingredients

- 6 ounces stout
- 1 ounce Irish cream
- 1 ounce chocolate syrup

SERVES 1

Perfect Pairing

Try this cocktail crafted with complementary alcohol. It's a match made in heaven.

Pour ingredients into a lowball glass and stir to combine. Add enough ice to fill the glass. Yum! Who knew so much flavor could be packed into such a little glass?

IRISH STOUT TREATS

Ingredients

- **3 tablespoons butter**
- **5 cups miniature marshmallows**
- **⅓ cup Irish cream**
- **6 cups crisped rice cereal**
- **½ cup stout**
- **1 tablespoon whiskey**
- **¼ cup dark chocolate chips**
- **2 cups powdered sugar**
- **1 teaspoon unsweetened cocoa powder**

MAKES 15

1. Spray a 9″ x 13″ pan with cooking spray.

2. Melt the butter in a saucepan over low heat. Add the marshmallows and stir until melted. Remove from the heat; add the Irish cream and stir until mixed. Add the crisped rice cereal and stir until completely coated.

3. Press the cereal mixture into the greased pan and place in the refrigerator to cool for at least 20 minutes.

4. Meanwhile, heat the stout and whiskey in a small saucepan over medium heat until reduced by about half. Add the chocolate chips and stir until melted.

5. Put the powdered sugar and cocoa powder into a small bowl and add the stout reduction, one tablespoon at a time, and whisk until it reaches the consistency of a thick glaze that can be drizzled onto the treats. (You might not use all the stout reduction.)

6. Drizzle the treats with the stout glaze and cut into squares.

IRISH ICED LATTE

Ingredients

- **2 ounces cold coffee**
- **6 ounces stout**
- **½ ounce whiskey**
- **1 ounce simple syrup**
- **1 ounce heavy cream**

Mix coffee, stout, whiskey, and simple syrup in a highball glass. Add enough ice to fill the glass. Gently drizzle the heavy cream into the glass so it slowly sinks into coffee.

To make simple syrup, combine equal amounts sugar and water in a small saucepan over medium heat until the sugar dissolves. Cool before using.

SERVES 1

Stout

SERVES
4

TIRAMI-BREW

Ingredients

- **1 (8 ounce) package cream cheese, softened**
- **2 cups whipped topping, thawed**
- **½ cup stout**
- **½ cup brewed coffee**
- **Vanilla wafers**
- **½ to 1 teaspoon cocoa powder**

1. With an electric mixer, whip the cream cheese and gently fold in the whipped topping.

2. In a shallow pie dish or bowl, stir together stout and coffee. Quickly dip a few vanilla wafers into the coffee mixture and place in the bottom of an individual serving dish or cup.

3. Carefully spread 2 heaping spoonfuls of the cream cheese mixture on top of the soaked wafers; sprinkle with cocoa powder.

4. Repeat two more times to make three layers, but on the final layer add just a light dusting of cocoa powder on top. Repeat the process for each individual dish.

SMOKY PECAN PIE BROWNIES

Coffee Stout

MAKES 12

Ingredients

- 18 whole graham cracker rectangles
- 1 tablespoon plus 1 cup brown sugar, divided
- 1 ¼ cups melted butter, divided
- 2 cups sugar
- 1 ½ cups unsweetened cocoa powder
- 2 teaspoons sea salt, divided
- ¾ cup plus 2 tablespoons coffee stout
- 1 teaspoon plus 1 tablespoon vanilla, divided
- 4 eggs plus 2 egg yolks, divided
- ⅔ cup flour
- ¾ teaspoon smoked paprika
- ½ cup light corn syrup
- ¼ cup heavy cream
- 2 cups pecans, coarsely chopped

1. Preheat the oven to 350°. Crush the graham crackers and mix with 2 tablespoons of the brown sugar and ½ cup butter. Press the mixture evenly into the bottom of a 9″ x 13″ baking pan and set aside.

2. In a bowl, stir together the sugar, cocoa powder, 1 teaspoon sea salt, ½ cup butter, ¾ cup coffee stout, and 1 teaspoon vanilla. Add 2 of the eggs and the 2 egg yolks and stir to combine.

3. Stir in the flour and paprika and then spread the mixture evenly over the crust. Bake for 20 minutes; remove from the oven and cool for 20 minutes. Reduce the oven temperature to 325°.

4. Grab a clean bowl and mix the remaining 1 cup brown sugar, ¼ cup butter, 2 tablespoons beer, and 2 eggs; stir in the syrup, cream, and pecans.

5. Pour this evenly over the partially baked brownie layer, sprinkle with the remaining 1 teaspoon sea salt, and bake 40 to 50 minutes longer. The center will still be a little bit jiggly. Cool to room temperature, cover, and chill until set.

Stout

CHOCOLATE-GUINNESS FLOAT

Ingredients

- 2 scoops chocolate ice cream
- Chilled stout (Guinness)

SERVES 1

Place the ice cream in a mug. Fill with chilled stout. That's it! Simple and delicious.

TRY A BOURBON-GINGER BEER FLOAT:

2 scoops of vanilla ice cream and 2 ounces bourbon topped off with chilled ginger beer.

Stout

SERVES
5

NO-CHURN TOFFEE & STOUT ICE CREAM

Ingredients

- **1 ½ cups heavy cream**
- **⅓ cup granulated sugar**
- **½ cup powdered sugar**
- **3 tablespoons cocoa powder**
- **½ teaspoon salt**
- **½ cup toffee bits**
- **¼ cup stout**

1. Add heavy cream, granulated sugar, and powdered sugar to a mixing bowl. Beat together on high until soft peaks form.

2. Add cocoa powder, salt, and toffee bits and mix until combined.

3. While the mixer is running, slowly pour the stout into the bowl and mix until well combined. Transfer to a freezer-safe container and freeze until set, about 7 hours.

NO-CHURN BOURBON ICE CREAM

Ingredients

- 2 tablespoons butter
- 4 cups fresh or frozen pitted tart cherries
- 2 tablespoons brown sugar
- 2 tablespoons bourbon
- 2 cups heavy cream
- 1 (14 ounce) can sweetened condensed milk
- Seeds from 1 vanilla bean (or 1 teaspoon vanilla)
- 1 cup mini chocolate chips

MAKES 1½ QUARTS

1. Melt the butter in a big skillet over medium-high heat. Add the cherries and brown sugar and bring to a boil.

2. Boil for several minutes, until the liquid reduces to just a few tablespoons. Take the skillet off the heat and stir in the bourbon. Set aside until cool.

3. In a chilled mixing bowl, combine heavy cream, sweetened condensed milk, and vanilla. Beat until stiff peaks form.

4. Carefully stir in mini chocolate chips along with the cooled cherries and cherry juice.

5. Transfer the mixture to a lidded freezer-safe container and freeze at least 4 hours.

BOOZY CHERRIES

Ingredients

- ¾ cup bourbon
- 2½ tablespoons sugar
- 1 cup frozen sweet cherries

1. In a small saucepan over low heat, simmer bourbon with sugar until sugar dissolves; remove from the heat and let stand 15 minutes.

2. Pack thawed cherries in a lidded glass jar and pour syrup over the fruit to cover. Cover tightly and store in the refrigerator.

3. Serve over cake or ice cream or in beverages for a sweet little kick.

MAKES 1 CUP

Bourbon

SERVES
12

PUMPKIN BOURBON CHEESECAKE

Ingredients

- ¼ cup, unsalted butter, melted and cooled
- ¾ cup graham cracker crumbs
- ½ cup pecans, finely chopped
- ¾ cup brown sugar, divided
- ¾ cup plus 3½ tablespoons sugar, divided
- 1½ cups pumpkin puree
- 3 eggs
- 1 teaspoon vanilla
- 2 tablespoons plus ¾ cup heavy cream, divided
- 3 tablespoons plus 2 teaspoons bourbon, divided
- 1 tablespoon cornstarch
- 2½ teaspoons cinnamon
- 1 teaspoon ground nutmeg
- 1 teaspoon ground ginger
- ¼ teaspoon ground cloves
- ½ teaspoon salt
- 3 (8 ounce) packages cream cheese, softened
- 2 cups sour cream
- Pecan halves, optional

1. Mix butter, crumbs, pecans, and ¼ cup each brown sugar and sugar; press firmly onto the bottom and ½ inch up the sides of a greased 9-inch springform pan. Chill 1 hour.

2. Preheat the oven to 350°. Whisk together the pumpkin, eggs, vanilla, 2 tablespoons cream, and 2 tablespoons bourbon; set aside.

3. In a large mixing bowl, mix the cornstarch, cinnamon, nutmeg, ginger, cloves, salt, ½ cup sugar, and the remaining ½ cup brown sugar. Add the cream cheese and beat until smooth. Add the set-aside pumpkin mixture and beat until combined. Pour the filling into the chilled crust and smooth the top.

4. Set on a rimmed baking sheet and place in the oven. Bake for 50 to 60 minutes or until just set. Remove pans from the oven and set on a cooling rack for 5 minutes. Don't turn off the oven.

5. Mix the sour cream, 2 tablespoons sugar, and 1 tablespoon bourbon until smooth; spread evenly over the cheesecake. Return pans to oven and bake 3 minutes. Turn off oven, but leave the cheesecake inside for 3 hours or until cool. Cover and chill for 4 hours before removing the sides of the pan.

6. Beat together the remaining ¾ cup cream, 1½ tablespoons sugar, and 2 teaspoons bourbon until stiff peaks form; use to frost cheesecake as desired. Garnish with pecan halves.

SERVES 18

BOURBON APPLE CAKE

Ingredients

- 4 cups baking apples, peeled and coarsely chopped
- ¾ cup walnuts, coarsely chopped
- 1 cup plus 2 teaspoons bourbon, divided
- ½ cup vegetable oil
- 2 eggs, beaten
- 2¼ cups sugar, divided

- 2 cups flour
- 2 teaspoons baking soda
- 2 teaspoons cinnamon
- 1 teaspoon salt
- 1 teaspoon ground nutmeg
- ¼ teaspoon ground cloves
- 2 cups whipping cream

1. Soak the apples and walnuts in 1 cup bourbon for 1 hour, stirring occasionally. After an hour, preheat the oven to 350° and grease a 9″ x 13″ baking pan.

2. In a large bowl, stir together the oil, eggs, and 2 cups of the sugar. In a separate bowl, mix the flour, baking soda, cinnamon, salt, nutmeg, and cloves. Add the dry ingredients to the wet ingredients and stir to combine.

3. Pour the apples and walnuts along with the soaking liquid into the batter, stirring to blend. Transfer the batter to the prepped pan and bake for 45 to 50 minutes or until the cake tests done.

4. While the cake cools, pour the whipping cream into a chilled bowl and beat on high, using chilled beaters, gradually beating in the remaining ¼ cup sugar and 2 teaspoons bourbon until stiff peaks form. Serve with the cake.

BOURBON CARAMEL CORN CRUNCH

Ingredients

- **6 cups popcorn, popped**
- **Salted peanuts**
- **6 tablespoons butter**
- **⅓ cup dark brown sugar**
- **3 tablespoons light corn syrup**
- **¼ teaspoon salt**
- **1 teaspoon vanilla**
- **¼ cup bourbon**

1. Preheat the oven to 300°. Line a rimmed baking sheet with parchment paper.

2. Add the popcorn and a handful of salted peanuts to a big bowl.

3. In a medium saucepan over medium heat, combine butter, dark brown sugar, corn syrup, and salt until it comes to a boil, stirring often.

4. Boil for 5 minutes, stirring constantly.

5. Remove the pan from the heat and stir in vanilla and bourbon; pour over the popcorn and stir to coat.

6. Spread mixture onto prepped baking sheet and sprinkle with extra salt if you'd like. Bake for 35 minutes, stirring once.

7. Remove from oven and let stand about 15 minutes. Enjoy!

MAKES 7 CUPS

Bourbon

MAKES ABOUT 36

BOURBON BALLS

Ingredients

- **3 cups vanilla wafer crumbs**
- **1 cup finely ground pecans**
- **1 cup powdered sugar**

- **1½ tablespoons unsweetened cocoa powder**
- **3 tablespoons light corn syrup**
- **½ cup bourbon**

1. Stir together vanilla wafer crumbs, pecans, powdered sugar, and cocoa powder. Add corn syrup and bourbon and stir well.

2. Form into 1¼-inch balls and roll in powdered or granulated sugar or crushed pecans.

3. Set aside for an hour and roll again if using sugars. Store tightly covered in the fridge.

VANILLA BOURBON CUPCAKES

Ingredients

- **1 (15.25 ounce) package French vanilla cake mix**
- **½ cup vegetable oil**
- **3 eggs**
- **¾ cup water**
- **¼ cup plus ⅓ cup bourbon, divided**

- **1 cup butter, softened**
- **7½ cups powdered sugar**
- **⅓ cup whole milk**
- **1 tablespoon vanilla**

1. Mix together the cake mix, oil, eggs, water, and ¼ cup bourbon in a mixing bowl. Divide the batter among 24 lined muffin cups and bake until cupcakes test done; cool.

2. For the frosting, beat butter until creamy. Gradually add powdered sugar, ⅓ cup bourbon, and milk until blended. Stir in vanilla. Frost cupcakes and enjoy.

Bourbon

MAKES
24

BOURBON CHOCO-SICLES

Ingredients

- ½ cup sugar
- 3 ounces bittersweet baking chocolate, chopped
- 2 tablespoons unsweetened cocoa powder
- ⅛ teaspoon salt
- 2 cups water
- 2 tablespoons bourbon

SERVES 8

1. In a large saucepan over medium heat, mix sugar, chocolate, cocoa powder, salt, and water.
2. Bring to a boil, whisking constantly.
3. Remove from heat; cool 30 minutes. Stir in bourbon and pour into popsicle molds.
4. Add a popsicle stick to each mold and freeze overnight. Enjoy!

ICE CREAM MANHATTAN

Ingredients

- ½ cup heavy cream
- 2¼ teaspoons sweet vermouth
- 1½ teaspoons sugar
- Angostura bitters
- Vanilla ice cream
- ¾ ounce bourbon
- 1 tablespoon maraschino cherry juice
- Cherry soda
- Whipped cream
- Cherries

SERVES 2

1. Chill two large glasses.
2. Beat heavy cream until frothy; add sweet vermouth, sugar, and a dash of Angostura bitters and beat until soft peaks form. Chill.
3. Place 2 or 3 scoops of ice cream into the chilled glasses and add bourbon and maraschino cherry juice to each glass. Fill with cold cherry soda and top with the prepped whipped cream and a cherry.

INDEX